TH
PSYCHOPAT

CURR

THE

PSYCHOPATH INSIDE

A NEUROSCIENTIST'S PERSONAL
JOURNEY INTO THE DARK SIDE
OF THE BRAIN

JAMES FALLON

CURRENT

CURRENT
Published by the Penguin Group
Penguin Group (USA) LLC
375 Hudson Street
New York, New York 10014

USA I Canada I UK I Ireland I Australia I New Zealand I India I South Africa I China
penguin.com
A Penguin Random House Company

First published by Current, a member of Penguin Group (USA) LLC, 2013

Photographs by the author.

ISBN 978-1-59184-600-0

Printed in the United States of America
1   3   5   7   9   10   8   6   4   2

Set in Janson Text LT Std
Designed by Alissa Amell

Penguin is committed to publishing works of quality and integrity.
In that spirit, we are proud to offer this book to our readers; however, the story,
the experiences, and the words are the author's alone.

To my parents, Jennie and John Henry, who recognized my true nature very early on, and nurtured it anyway

CONTENTS

CONTENTS

THE
PSYCHOPATH INSIDE

One October day in 2005, as the last vestiges of an Indian summer moved across Southern California, I was inputting some last-minute changes into a paper I was planning to submit to the *Ohio State Journal of Criminal Law*. I had titled it "Neuroanatomical Background to Understanding the Brain of a Young Psychopath" and based it on a long series of analyses I had performed, on and off for a decade, of individual brain scans of psychopathic murderers. These are some of the baddest dudes you can imagine—they'd done some heinous things over the years, things that would make you cringe if I didn't have to adhere to confidentiality agreements and could tell you about them.

But their pasts weren't the only things that separated them from the rest of us. As a neuroscientist well into the fourth decade of my career, I'd looked at a lot of brain scans over the years, and these had been different. The brains belonging to these killers shared a rare and alarming pattern of low brain function in certain parts of the frontal and temporal lobes—areas commonly associated with self-control and empathy. This makes sense for those with a history of inhuman violence, since the reduction of activity in these regions suggests a lack of a normal sense of moral reasoning and of the ability to inhibit their impulses. I explained this pattern in my paper, submitted it for publication, and turned my attention to the next project.

At the same time I'd been studying the murderers' scans, my lab had been conducting a separate study exploring which genes, if any, are linked to Alzheimer's disease. As part of our research, my colleagues and I had run genetic tests and taken brain scans of several Alzheimer's patients as well as several members of my family, who were serving as the normal control group.

On this same October day, I sat down to analyze my family's scans and noticed that the last scan in the pile was strikingly odd. In fact it looked exactly like the most abnormal of the scans I had just been writing about, suggesting that the poor individual it belonged to was a psychopath—or at least shared an uncomfortable amount of traits with one. Not suspicious of any of my family members, I naturally assumed that their scans had somehow been mixed with the other pile on the table. I generally have a lot of research going on at one time, and even though I try to keep my work organized it was entirely possible for things to get misplaced. Unfortunately, since we were trying to keep the scans anonymous, we'd coded them to hide the names of the individuals they belonged to. To be sure I hadn't made a mistake, I asked our lab technician to break the blind code.

When I found out who the scan belonged to, I had to believe there was a mistake. In a fit of pique, I asked the technician to check the scanner and all the notes from the other imaging and database technicians. But there had been no mistake.

The scan was mine.

Imagine with me for a moment.

It's a bright, warm Saturday morning and you decide to take a stroll through the park near your home. After a brisk walk, you sit down on a bench in the shade of an oak tree next to a nice-enough-looking chap. You say hi, and he says hi, and then he says what a nice day it is and how good it is to be alive. As you talk to him for the next fifteen minutes, you form an opinion of him as he forms an opinion of you. There is much you can glean from someone in this brief window of time. You might learn what he does for a living, whether he is married or has children, or what he likes to do in his spare time. He can appear to be intelligent, charming, open, funny, and a generally pleasant conversationalist who can tell an interesting little story.

But depending on who this person is, the second fifteen minutes can be dramatically more telling. For instance, if he is in the early stages of Alzheimer's disease, he might repeat the same exact interesting little story, with the same exact facial and body movements and punch line as before. If he is schizophrenic, he might start to shift in his seat or lean in a little too close as he talks to you. You might start to feel uncomfortable and will get up and leave, glancing back to make sure he isn't following you.

If I were the man sitting next to you on the bench, you would probably find me a generally interesting person. If you asked me what line of work I'm in, I'd say that I am a brain researcher, and if you pressed further I'd say I am a professor in the Department of Psychiatry and Human Behavior and affiliated with the Department of Anatomy and Neurobiology in the School of Medicine at the University of California, Irvine. I'd tell you how I've spent my career teaching medical students and residents and graduate students about the brain. If you seemed interested, I would then tell you about my research with adult stem cells and animal models of Parkinson's disease and chronic stroke, and that the basic research from my lab has led to the creation of three biotech companies, one of which has been netting profits consistently for the past twenty-five years, and another that just won a national award from its peer biotech companies.

If you still seemed interested, I might mention that I am also involved in organizations and think tanks that focus on the arts, architecture, music, education, and medical research, or that I have served as an adviser to the U.S. Department of Defense on what war does to the brain. If you asked further, I might mention the TV shows and films I've acted in or that I thoroughly enjoyed my past jobs as a bartender, a laborer, a schoolteacher, and a carpenter, and still have my out-of-active-duty Teamsters' card from my days as a truck driver.

At some point you might start thinking to yourself that I'm a blowhard or even that I am making this stuff up, especially if I also mentioned that when I was fourteen years old I was named Catholic Boy of the Year for the diocese of Albany, New York, or was a five-sport high school and college athlete. But although you might think I talk way too much or am something of a bullshitter, you would also find that when I talk with you, I look you in the eye and listen carefully to everything you say. In fact, you might be surprised at how interested I am in your life, your opinions, and how you view the world.

If you agreed to meet me again, we might end up becoming friends. Over time, you might notice things about me that rub you the wrong way—I may occasionally be caught in a lie, or I might disappoint you from time to time by not showing up at an event you invite me to. But despite my mild narcissism and regular bouts of selfishness, we'd probably have fun together. Because, at the end of the day, I am basically a regular guy.

Except for one thing. I'm a borderline psychopath.

I agreed to write this story, a true if not wholly complete story, in part to share with my family, friends, and colleagues the biological and psychological background of my family. By necessity, this exposition is based on comprehensive scientific data from brain imaging, genetics, and psychiatry, but also emerges from brutally honest and sometimes disturbing admissions and discussions about myself and my past. (I hope my family doesn't disown me once they're done reading.) My aim here is not simply to tell a story or to espouse some new scientific findings. I hope that by telling my story, I will illuminate the conversation surrounding a subject that has received a lot of attention in our culture despite a general lack of understanding and consensus: psychopathy.

Beyond the basic science and personal story, I hope that the research I've done and the theories I've put forth about the way our brains, genes, and early environment determine how likely we are to be psychopaths might be useful, not only to individual readers, but also within the larger realms of parenting and criminal law. As strange as it sounds, the science discussed in the following pages could even help us achieve world peace. I've hypothesized that in areas with chronic violence, from Gaza to East L.A., the concentration of genes associated with psychopathy might be increasing as women mate with bad boys for protection and aggressive genes spread, increasing the violence and repeating the loop. Over generations, we end up with warrior societies. It's a speculative idea but one that's important to consider and study further.

I'm a committed scientist—a neuroscientist who studies the anatomy and function of the brain—and this fact has shaped the way I view behavior, motivation, and morality for my entire adult life. In my mind, we are machines, albeit machines we don't understand all that well, and I have believed for decades that we have very little control over what we do and who we are. To me, nature (genetics) determines about 80 percent of our personality and behavior, and nurture (how and in what environment we are raised) only 20 percent.

This is the way I have always thought about the brain and behavior. But this understanding took a stinging, and rather embarrassing, blow starting about 2005, and I continue to reconcile my past belief with my present reality. I have come to understand—even more than I did before—that humans are, by nature, complicated creatures. And to reduce our actions, motivations, desires, and needs to absolutes is doing each of us a disservice. We are not simply good or evil, right or wrong, kind or vindictive, benign or dangerous. We are not simply the product of biology, either, and science can only tell us part of the story.

Which brings me back to the story at hand.

CHAPTER 1

What Is a Psychopath?

"What is a psychopath?"

After viewing my brain scan—which, being a scientist, I considered more of a professional curiosity than a personal cause for alarm—I started asking my psychiatrist colleagues this question to see if I fit the bill. I asked some of the most preeminent researchers in the field, and yet I couldn't seem to get a satisfactory answer. Several dismissed the question, saying psychopaths didn't exist at all and that asking them to define *psychopath* was like asking them to define a nervous breakdown. It's a phrase people throw around, but it doesn't bear any scientific or professional meaning. (The same goes for *vegetable*, which is a somewhat arbitrary culinary term, not a biological one.) When I asked my friend Fabio Macciardi, a UCI colleague and a noted psychiatrist, he said, "There is no psychiatric diagnosis of *psychopath*." After some pressing he explained, "The closest thing we have in the manual is a personality disorder, antisocial personality disorder. But that is not always the animal you're looking for, either."

The manual Fabio was referring to is the *Diagnostic and Sta-*

tistical Manual of Mental Disorders, most commonly referred to as the DSM. For psychiatrists and psychologists, this is the Bible—the book that outlines, defines, and classifies all disorders of the mind as agreed upon by the American Psychiatric Association and provides a standard of diagnosis that professionals are expected to follow. The DSM classifies a wide range of disorders from anorexia to schizophrenia, but psychopathy is not one of them. The definition for antisocial personality disorder, which Macciardi pointed to, is described as "a pervasive pattern of disregard for and violation of the rights of others that has been occurring in the person since the age of 15 years, as indicated by three (or more) of seven criteria, namely: a failure to conform to social norms; irresponsibility; deceitfulness; indifference to the welfare of others; recklessness; a failure to plan ahead; and irritability and aggressiveness." Outside of the DSM, many doctors and researchers have their own definitions of what makes a psychopath. The problem is, every definition is different and none are cut-and-dried.

If one considers conventional medical standards of diagnosis, it's actually no wonder there is so much controversy surrounding psychopathy. For conditions like obesity, diabetes, and high blood pressure, it's easy to figure out whether a patient is afflicted, since the symptoms of these diseases are well-known and easy to test for. Do you have low levels of insulin, inhibiting your body's ability to metabolize sugar? You have diabetes. The same cannot be said for diseases of the mind.

For one thing, psychiatric diseases are not considered diseases at all. Diseases are based on knowledge of the cause (or etiology) of a particular disorder and the effects (or pathophysiology) they have on the body. Unlike for many true diseases of other organ systems, we don't have this luxury with diseases of the mind since so little is known of the underlying pathological biological mechanisms at work. Despite advances in our understanding of how the brain works, the organ is still largely a mystery to us. Therefore, most psychiatric problems are called disorders or syndromes. Psychopathy stands on the lowest rung of this disease-disorder ladder, since no one agrees on what defines it—or if it exists at all—and so there is no professional agreement as to the underlying causes. Trying to identify or define psychopathy with just a checklist of traits and no cause is like using a field taxonomy guide. If it flies and eats and makes noises it could be a bird, but it could also be a bat or an insect; you haven't nailed down what the thing really is.

Although there are no set methods to test for psychiatric disorders like psychopathy, we can determine some facets of a patient's mental state by studying his brain with imaging techniques like PET (positron emission tomography) and fMRI (functional magnetic resonance imaging) scanning, as well as genetics, behavioral and psychometric testing, and other pieces of information gathered from a full medical and psychiatric workup. Taken together, these tests can reveal symptoms that might indicate a psychiatric disorder. Since psychiatric disorders are often characterized by more than one symptom, a patient will be diagnosed based on the number and severity of various symptoms. For most disorders, a diagnosis is also classified on a sliding scale—

more often called a spectrum—that indicates whether the patient's case is mild, moderate, or severe. The most common spectrum associated with such disorders is the autism spectrum. At the low end are delayed language learning and narrow interests, and at the high end are strongly repetitive behaviors and an inability to communicate.

Despite the debate about whether psychopathy is a real disorder and, if so, what defines it, there are some accepted parameters within the medical community. The most famous and widely used test is the PCL-R (Psychopathy Checklist, Revised), also known as the Psychopath Test or Hare's Checklist, named for the Canadian psychiatrist Robert Hare, who developed it. The PCL-R consists of twenty items, each of which is scored 0, 1, or 2, designating whether the psychopathic trait is not present (0 points), partially present (1 point), or definitely present (2 points). A person with a "perfect" score of 40 is a full-blown, categorical psychopath on this scale. Thirty is the normal cutoff for a diagnosis, although sometimes 25 is used. The test is scored by a person trained in giving the scale, usually during a session in which the clinician interviews the subject, sometimes supplemented with legal and medical records and third-person references. An evaluation can also be made by someone who knows the subject well, without his being present.

The traits can be sorted into four different categories, or "factors." The interpersonal factor includes the traits of superficiality, grandiosity, and deceitfulness. The affective factor includes lack of remorse, lack of empathy, and refusal to accept responsibility for one's actions. The behavioral factor includes impulsivity, lack of goals, and unreliability. And the antisocial factor includes hotheadedness, a history of juvenile delinquency, and a criminal record. Antisocial personality disorder is related to psychopathy but is much more common and is a measure of outward disruptive behavior rather than an underlying personality problem. Psychopathy scores are actually a better predictor of criminal recidivism, severity, and premeditation.

Psychopathy is not something one can just casually assess, although there are versions of the test that can be self-administered and are not "officially" diagnostic. A typical statement on a self-administered checklist might be, "I can be shrewd, crafty, sly, and clever—if needed, I can also be deceptive, unscrupulous, underhanded, manipulative, and dishonest." Two other sample statements would be, "At times, I feel a strong need for novel, thrilling, and exciting stimulation; I get bored easily. This might result in me taking chances and doing things that are risky. Carrying tasks through 'to the bitter end' or staying in the same job for a longer time can feel very difficult for me," and "Significant amounts of the money I have made, I have made by intentionally exploiting or manipulating others. With 'classic' forms of work, I often feel a lack of motivation, a problem with my self-discipline, or an inability to complete my responsibilities."

To illustrate the degrees represented on the PCL-R, I like to point to pop culture, which is full of portrayals—some accurate, some less so—of psychopaths. The most extreme and ridiculous examples can be found in horror films featuring foul-toothed characters with one foggy eyeball who exude danger and immediately evoke chills. Think Freddy Krueger or the family in *The Texas Chain Saw Massacre*. Even Patrick Bateman, Christian Bale's self-loving, unhinged character in the film adaptation of *American Psycho*, is not representative of a true psychopath, as he is too violent to be realistic. These are caricatures—even the most violent criminals are rarely so obviously insane.

Some reasonable characterizations include Tommy DeVito, played by Joe Pesci in *Goodfellas*, and Frank Booth, played by Dennis Hopper in *Blue Velvet*. Both of these are relatively normal-looking guys—guys you might pass on the street and not think twice about. But they are deeply disturbed individuals who ultimately cannot control their innate aggressiveness and show little regret or sympathy for their violent actions. Tommy and Frank would score high on the PCL-R. Tommy in particular expresses the interpersonal aspects of glibness, charm, and manipulation. He's entertaining, and he can go in and out of character. In the "Do I amuse you?" exchange, he has the other guy pinned—there's no right answer. Psychopaths can put people into untenable positions. There's also a scene in which Tommy shoots a guy in the foot, then curses him out for making a big deal of it and goes back to playing cards. After a murder, psychopaths often say they feel like someone else did it, or the victim precipitated the pulling of the trigger. They feel detached, impelled to action by forces out of their control. Tommy calls the foot-shooting incident an "accident." Not all psychopaths are impulsive or physically violent, but some are, as in the cases of Tommy and Frank.

My favorite example comes from the 1986 film *Manhunter*, starring Brian Cox and William Petersen. Cox plays Hannibal Lecter, a cannibalistic serial killer who was later reprised more famously by Anthony Hopkins in the films *The Silence of the Lambs* and *Hannibal*. Lecter is characterized by his lack of empathy, his glib and charming manipulation of people, and his utter lack of remorse for his horrid and perverse behaviors. In short, he is what many would consider a classic psychopath and would probably have scored high on Hare's Checklist. Real-life psychopaths who resemble Lecter account for the more sensational and extreme cases—think Jeffrey Dahmer, Ted Bundy, or the Son of Sam.

But according to Hare, there is an entire other category of psychopaths out there—those who don't score as high on the PCL-R but who still exhibit strong signs of classic psychopathic traits. These are people like the hero of *Manhunter*, the FBI profiler Will Graham, played by Petersen. Graham recognizes that he has the same urges and lack of interpersonal empathy as Lecter. Although he is not a murderer, he is, in fact, a psychopath, or at least a near-psychopath, what I like to call Psychopath Lite. He might score a 15 or 23 on the PCL-R, just under the 30-point score cutoff for full psychopathy, but other than that, you might think him completely normal. When my wife, Diane, and I saw the film in 1986, she pointed to Will and said, "That is you." (At the time, it threw me off a bit, but I decided she was referring to how nice and deep a guy Will was.)

Full-blown, categorical psychopaths—those who score 30 or more—make up only about 1 percent of females and 3 percent of males who have taken the test. But despite—or perhaps because of—its broad classification system, Hare's scale has been hotly contested, as usually happens in a new field of medicine or science. Every scientific meeting, every casual conversation in hallways and bars among colleagues in widely divergent fields, inevitably leads to an argument over the nature of the condition.

One critique is that the scale doesn't take into consideration class and ethnicity. What's normative behavior in a crime-ridden lower-class neighborhood in downtown L.A. is different from that in an upper-class neighborhood in Minnesota. There are also debates about how well it predicts violence. Märta Wallinius and collaborators at the Swedish universities of Lund, Gothenburg, and Uppsala showed in 2012 that the antisocial facet (hotheadedness, etc.) predicts violent behavior particularly well, but the interpersonal aspect (superficiality, etc.) doesn't predict it at all. The criminal justice system is especially interested in such findings.

Despite the controversy over whether psychopaths exist, psychiatrists generally agree that one of the defining characteristics of those we refer to as psychopaths is the lack of interpersonal empathy, what one might call a flat emotional playing field. Psychopaths may not hate, but they also may not love the way most of us would prefer to love and be loved. Psychopaths are usually manipulative, are champion liars, and can be quite glib and disarmingly charming. They don't fear consequences the way most people do, and while they may react to the stress of being caught in a lie or violent act like anyone would, some remain cool as cucumbers. Even the most dangerous can appear jovial, carefree, and social at times, but sooner or later they will display a telling distance, a quiet coldheartedness and disregard for others. They are often impulsive, yet lack guilt and remorse, meaning they may invite you to join in on their reckless, even dangerous fun, and then shrug their shoulders if someone gets hurt.

In identifying a psychopath, the Hare Checklist is a good start, but it's not perfect. Rather than adding up twenty traits, each with a value of 0, 1, or 2, I would score them each from 0 to 5, and use a mathematical model to give each trait a different weight. Even better, each person would have an individualized profile rather than a single numerical score or a categorical yes-or-no diagnosis. You can't judge health or obesity on height and weight alone. Are you exercising? What are you eating and drinking? You can be overweight but in great shape. A doctor who knows you well would take all of that into account.

It's also difficult to summarize a collection of behaviors as one disorder. There's a lot of overlap between conditions, such as histrionic, narcissistic, and antisocial personality disorders. And everyone is a little bit psychopathic and has a little bit of ADHD and so on. Psychiatry is moving away from categorical thinking—the latest diagnostic manual talks about "dimensions" to disorders—but it's hard when doctors don't want to learn new methods, insurance companies need to rely on specific diagnoses, and everyone likes closure and clearly defined labels. I see psychopathy like others see art; I can't define it, but I know it when I see it.

One question people often ask is if there is a difference between a sociopath and a psychopath. Barring the fact that many psychologists deny the existence of either, in a clinical setting the difference is purely semantic. Robert Hare has pointed out that sociologists are more likely to focus on the environmental or socially modifiable facets of the disorder, so prefer the term *sociopathy*, whereas psychologists and psychiatrists prefer to include the genetic, cognitive, and emotional factors as well as the social factors when making a diagnosis, and therefore would opt for *psychopathy*. Since I am a brain scientist and am interested in the genetic and neurological causes of this personality disorder, I will use the term *psychopath* for the purposes of this book. And I will use it to describe people with some combination of those four facets of the Hare Checklist: interpersonal, affective, behavioral, and antisocial traits.

I have been interested in the brain ever since I saw the movie *Charly* when I was a junior in college in 1968. It is a story about an intellectually handicapped man who has the will to change his life and to learn how to learn. And learn he does, temporarily becoming a genius after undergoing a new neurosurgical procedure, the same procedure done to his alter ego, a laboratory mouse. This prescient film on the biological and chemical basis of behavior provided a clear career direction for me.

Throughout my career, I have studied many facets of the brain. Whereas most researchers tend to specialize in a relatively narrow field of study, my interests have covered all manner of territory—from stem cells to sleep deprivation.

I started studying psychopathy in the 1990s, when I was asked by my colleagues in the Department of Psychiatry and Human Behavior at the University of California, Irvine, to analyze PET scans of particularly violent murderers, including serial killers, who had just been convicted in court, and were subsequently starting the penalty phase of their trials. It is during this stage of the legal process that a murderer typically agrees to undergo a brain scan, often in the hope that a finding of brain damage will lead to a more lenient sentence.

As I've already mentioned, we know very little about psychopathy, but without scanning technology, we'd probably know even less. It's easy for a psychopath to feign caring and remorse when his brain tells a different story. This is the work I'd been doing that October day in 2005, when I discovered my odd brain scan indicating reduced activity in areas responsible for empathy and ethics.

You might assume, given my closeness to the subject, that I'd be scared or worried or upset. But I wasn't because I knew better. I was a happily married man with three kids whom I loved dearly. I had never been violent or manipulative or committed a dangerous crime. I wasn't some Hannibal Lecter type—an esteemed brain scientist studying the minds of unsuspecting patients in an attempt to understand how I might be better able to control them for my benefit. Heck, I was a research scientist—I didn't even have patients!

But my brain scan did tell me something I hadn't fully understood before. I had just submitted a paper outlining the research I had done into the minds of psychopaths. I had laid out a theory describing the neuroanatomical basis of psychopathy and identi-fied a pattern that I myself matched. So how could I reconcile my brain with the findings I'd just reported? Was I really an exception to my own rule? If I wasn't a psychopath, what was I? And if we couldn't rely on studies of our own brains, the very organ respon-sible for every thought and action we have, how could we ever understand who we truly are?

CHAPTER 2

Evil Brewing

The media and pop culture have done a great job over the years painting pictures of psychopathic children or disturbed kids who grow up to be violent killers. Just consider every time there's a school shooting; afterward, the friends, family, classmates, and teachers of the individual responsible seem to notice all of the warning signs that should have predicted what was to come. When parents see signs of abnormal or antisocial behavior in their kids, they immediately call the doctor, hoping therapy or prescription meds will head off any danger at the pass.

That's one reason why I originally gave little thought to my brain scan. I had had a happy childhood, and it wasn't until I started reflecting on certain episodes in the context of my research and personal discovery that I started to see indications that I was not like the other boys.

I was born in Poughkeepsie, New York, at 7:07 a.m. on October 18, 1947, weighing seven pounds and seven ounces. Although I'm not a superstitious person, my lucky number by default has always been seven. The pregnancy was not a difficult one, but was angst-filled for my parents, who had already experienced four miscarriages leading up to my uneventful birth. According to what my parents, aunts and uncles, and grandparents have told me, I was a happy baby and toddler, but not so happy that I didn't drive my older brother, Jack, crazy with my crying.

According to my mother and several other family members, I was an "adorable happy baby" with no behavioral problems, although I developed severe, untreated asthma in my second year of life, a malady that follows me to this day. The difficulty breathing for days at a time would lead to some of my earliest and most lasting memories. I recently asked my mother to describe my personality until I hit puberty, and if my behavior changed or was strange in any way during this time. For adjectives, she said that throughout this period I was "adorable, lovable, straightforward, mischievous, inquisitive, capable, cheerful, insightful, likable, friendly, a prankster," and added, "a pain in the ass, take your pick."

Over the years my family members told me similar things about my childhood self. They told me I was a beautiful toddler, and that my grandfather even once entered me into a national toddler beauty contest. My father carried me everywhere we went together, and this bonding continued even into my preadolescent years when he would take me to bars with him to play pool and darts and shuffleboard games, and sit at the bar and talk to the owners. We would go on fishing trips together, including overnight stays in the Adirondacks. He started taking me to the Thoroughbred and harness tracks at Saratoga Springs starting in 1950, when I was three, and I have made it a point to go to the track in Saratoga every August since for sixty-three straight years, and to go trout fishing whenever possible. I was also close to my mother, and learned how to cook and sew and iron from her at a very early age.

My family moved from Poughkeepsie in 1951, when I was four, and I started kindergarten the next year at St. Patrick's School in Cohoes, New York. A Catholic primary school taught by nuns, it provided a happy time without incident. Well, there was one incident. While practicing to make my First Communion in first grade, I started joking around and my teacher put me into a trash basket, butt down, for fifteen minutes. Some of my classmates looked at me, feet up in the air, with fear in their eyes, while a couple of goofball guys held back laughs. I distinctly remember thinking the scene was funny, so I made some goofball faces back at my classmates, earning an additional fifteen minutes of hard time. I believe it was at that moment when I began my career as class clown, and it's a disposition I still can't shake. When I was fifty-eight, I got kicked out of a sensitivity class along with a well-known TV network newswoman with whom I was flirting and giggling while a serious touchy-feely session was going on with thirty other people. I swear she was one of the girls in my St. Patrick's first-grade class who got me into hot water with the nuns.

A few years later we moved from Cohoes to nearby, upscale Loudonville, where I attended fourth through sixth grades at Loudonville School. These three years at the end of my primary schooling were uniformly bright and wonderful. I remember many of the individual days from those years, and I flourished academically and socially. My teachers were particularly talented, and one, Miss Winnie Smith, has to be one of the greatest primary schoolteachers of all time. She was well liked by most of us, but treated me with particular attention, and encouraged me to act in school plays, to play musical instruments, to draw, and to partake in all social activities, which I did with such enjoyment that I can remember dozens of even the most mundane events throughout that fifth-grade year with her at the helm.

During my later primary school years I occasionally worked in my father and uncle's pharmacy in Troy. My early interests in the natural world, animals, gardening, the outdoors—fueled by a native aptitude for science, math, and engineering—provided me with a comfortable interaction with the pharmacists. I knew from a young age that I wanted to be a scientist. I was fascinated by what makes us who we are and why we are here. All the medical talk and sensory banquet one experiences working in the back rooms of a large pharmacy were incredible preparation for the future. It all fascinated me from the beginning, and I would continue working in the pharmacy in junior high school and high school. I was interested in all of the drugs, and the chemistry of the basic ingredients of the apothecary. Then I discovered the brown bottles of potassium nitrate, or saltpeter. After a few questions to the young pharmacists, I discovered that this compound was a key ingredient in gunpowder, probably something I didn't need to know. The pharmacy was well stocked with basic chemicals, and I quickly located the other ingredients: charcoal, sulfur, and an accelerant, magnesium oxide. This began a long love affair with explosives and all things that go boom. I started making my own fireworks and then graduated, with the help of a particularly daring friend, to making larger and larger pipe bombs, which we detonated on a regular basis for years. About the same time, two other friends with a penchant for starting fires and shooting guns invited me along on their adventures, which often ended in grand field fires that threatened to burn down their own houses. With two of these friends we would also try to act tough, but we were just mischievous boys, hardly malevolent, although if we tried getting away with that stuff today, we'd be in jail every week. Some of my friends were also into shooting animals with guns—nailing birds or pegging cows in the ass—but that never interested me.

We were hellions on nights sanctioned for mayhem, such as Halloween, my favorite holiday. We pulled off every prank imaginable but never hurt anyone, and at the end of the night, loaded down by bags chockablock full of candy, we would drop them off at the convent for charity, or maybe just to keep the nuns sweet the next time they had a reason for disciplining us. We were not bad kids, just pranksters. For me, the innate drive to tease and torment people may have a dark side, but the way it would ultimately express itself after the joke was over usually had a light side.

My penchant for such shenanigans may have been learned. My father and uncle were both pranksters, with my uncle Arnold, my father's pharmacy partner, and my maternal great-uncle Charlie being the masters. But in all cases their practical jokes ended on a positive note. My father and uncle would pretend to their poorer customers that they were price-gouging them, when in reality they were slashing their prices by up to 90 percent. If someone came in wanting to buy a cane that cost ten dollars, they'd give him a sly look instead of naming the real price and say, "That'll be two dollars." I would watch them do this time and time again, and the pranks, although they made these customers a bit crazy, were really done to ensure that the less-fortunate clientele could maintain their dignity without going broke.

As grade school became junior high and high school, I transitioned to Shaker High School, a public school in nearby Colonie. It was a new and experimental school and sported high-tech features such as computerization, even back in 1959. My years at Shaker were also uniformly terrific, and I was given every opportunity to flourish academically, socially, and in the arts, music, and sports. This was a tremendous school with some gifted teachers, and I loved every year there.

For my entire postpubescent life, I felt that I was a nice, regular guy—kind, helpful, and fun to be around. Although I said some curious things now and again, I was accepted by most people and found that they wanted to hang out with me, and that many people wanted to be my playmate and often close friend. I seemed to get along with girls and women better than most guys, and my numerous long-standing close friendships, from my teenage years to the present, provided proof that I was not only a man's man, but also one who could form close friendships with women.

Physically, I was not intimidating—just short of six feet tall and weighing between 180 and 220 pounds throughout high school and college—nor aggressive. I did not fight with people, and was one of the more calmly behaved of my siblings, who ranged from very introverted to very extroverted and who had a range of aggressive interactions with people throughout life. I have four brothers and a sister. Jack was born first, followed by me five years later. Four years after that came my brother Peter, followed three years later by Tom, then Mark two years later, and finally Carol the year after that. Pete was always a handful. He has ADHD and was climbing the walls and getting into mischief. Jack was more aggressive than I was and got into a lot of fights. Tom, Mark, Carol, and I were pretty calm.

I wasn't known as a fighter, but I'd go after a bully if I saw him picking on someone. I'd step in and tell him to stop. If I needed to, I'd muscle him and lift him off the ground and tell him I was going to kill him. This happened a number of times, starting when I was around twelve. One time when I was nineteen or twenty, I saw my buddy provoking a fight in a bar and I pulled him away, but the other guy went after him. I thought that wasn't fair, so I grabbed the guy by the scruff and yanked him outside. My friend wanted me to hold him while he hit him, but I thought that wasn't fair, either, so I refused. While many of the males in my family are athletic and several just love to fight, I never developed a taste for pugilism, preferring to mentally pummel someone than to do so using bare knuckles. Even in high school I couldn't get all psyched up for a wrestling match or football game, opting always to get to my opponent by just rattling him and making him laugh by any means necessary. I loved sports in this way, never serious or violent, but just good, romping fun.

While in junior high, I developed obsessive compulsive disorder (OCD), which manifested itself partially as an obsession with religion, in particular my mother's Catholicism. No one in my family or inner circle ever pushed me into religion, and I kept this as much to myself as possible. Only one priest, and my mother, seemed to notice the emerging obsession. I began to sneak off to daily Mass, and would spend every waking moment on Saturdays preparing to confess my sins on Saturday night, so that I could continue to take the sacraments on a daily basis. Throughout my entire youth, including my six years in junior high and high school, I never missed Sunday Mass or all the holy days of obligation. I lived in a secret world completely controlled by an internal mechanism of pointing out weaknesses in my character, and even in my perceptions. Always vigilant for purity and perfection, I began to make up sins that were quite bizarre. My priest tried to tell me in confession that what I was describing to him each week were not sins at all, and even though I knew they really weren't sins, I would mutate them into destructive ideations so that they became "sins."

It's not unusual for OCD sufferers to put a moral spin on their obsessions. One of my more bizarre drives was to pay as much attention to the left side of my personal space, extending outward to infinity, as to my right side. I would keep count of this internal space orientation, and at the end of each ten to twenty seconds of such internal dialogue, I would realize that I had spent one more second attending to one side than the other. That became a mortal sin. But then I would decide that thinking incorrectly like this would be another mortal sin on top of the first. At twelve years old, I could sit alone on a park bench, not moving, and commit forty mortal sins, each worthy of eternal damnation, in a one-hour period. This would continue for hours and days and dominated my inner life for two entire years. Generally I could hide the angst generated by this florid, obsessive-compulsive world, but it was eating me up, to be sure. At the same time, I was experiencing spontaneous moments of dread and doom lasting up to half an hour. These then became associated with an ongoing religious or, more correctly, spiritual crisis, that lasted for years. All of this occurred in the complete absence of any external pressure from family, friends, or church personnel. If anything, they tried to get me to chill out.

Aside from my attention to symmetry, I also had to wash my hands repeatedly. And walking to the school bus, I would waver thirty feet in each direction picking up litter, leaving a swath of cleanliness behind me. Everything became a moral issue. I had to be perfect, and I had to have good intentions about everything. If I did something good but it wasn't from the heart, I would start thinking that it was immoral. I knew it was crazy, but I couldn't put an end to it. Eventually I stopped telling people because they said it was insane. I couldn't even imagine stealing or breaking rules. I refused to have sex as a teenager, even when I was dating Diane, the woman who would become my wife, because I saw it as immoral. After several years she finally said enough is enough.

Years later, when I was in my sixties, my mother told me a story she remembers about my OCD. It was the summer of 1961.

I was thirteen years old and had been very social all my life. But suddenly, with no apparent trigger, I closed off and crawled into my own little world. I had nothing to do, but the guy next door had a beat-up old boat sitting in his yard. I looked at that and said maybe if I fix it up I could use it to go fishing. I retreated to work on the boat every day, sometimes for up to fourteen hours. I didn't talk to many people and I sank into a mood.

My mother told me that one day she watched me work on the boat from the kitchen window and grew concerned. It was the first time I'd ever exhibited any antisocial behavior. "I was torn whether to tell your father, and to contact a psychiatrist we knew," she said. By the time I started school in September and was forced into my routine, I went back to normal. My mother never told my father, and I never experienced another period of depression like that again. When I returned to school I became so active socially and athletically that anytime it would creep up, I'd have something to do. There wasn't any time to get depressed.

As I moved into my freshman year of high school, my piety was rewarded by my diocese naming me Catholic Boy of the Year at the yearly New York State conference of Catholic youth. For this honor, I got to spend some time with Governor Nelson Rockefeller, the Archbishop of New York Cardinal Spellman, and other officials of the Church and State. I met some other people about my age who had received the same honor. During the retreat associated with the statewide conference with these students and priests, I realized for the first time that my fellow Catholic youth activists were interested in action items of the Church, real practical matters, while I was just interested in a purely metaphysical world, a world of insanity.

My four years of high school were filled with nonstop activities. Every year I was on the football team, the wrestling team, and the track and field team. In the summer I swam competitively, and in the winter I skied competitively each year in slalom and giant slalom. Although I enjoyed victory as much as anyone else, I never got mad at opponents. The same could not be said of me in all competitive situations, however; when I played parlor games I proved to be perfectly obnoxious. I hated to lose, and after a while I ostracized any potential poker or Scrabble opponent in my circle of friends.

Despite my poor parlor sportsmanship, I was generally a nice guy. I was a musician in the band every year, acted in school productions, served as president of the drama club, and was involved in the student government. I enjoyed a rich social life and was considered one of the cool, good-looking, athletic, smart types in a school of more than a thousand students. I had three very close friends and about thirty people I considered good friends, and I was on friendly terms with all my classmates and was accepted into the jocks, thespians, arts, and geek groups. I sincerely felt at ease with all of them and found their interests and activities compelling. I had an exhausting sense of humor and an openness and optimism that made people want to spend time with me. I was a bright kid, but not particularly focused, and to my parents' dismay earned the distinction of "Class Clown" for my high school graduating class.

Recently I asked an old friend, Pat Quinn, whom I have known since the seventh grade and who later became a clinical psychologist, what she remembers of my personality and character while we were in high school. She e-mailed, "You were tough on the football field, but empathetic and caring off the field. You were a bright competitive student who seldom missed an opportunity to be a prankster. You also had a more conservative, rigid side when it came to politics and religion. As teenagers, it was not unusual to push the limits, particularly in the norms of the mid-sixties. But you were not a rule breaker and when it came to societal norms, you were clearly a black and white thinker. You could often be heard debating a popular subject, but you had little patience for those who were not of your intellectual ability. You were a well-rounded adolescent who would never be considered to lack insight, empathy, or compassion for others."

At the same time, in the background of my mind, I knew there was a dark bogeyman lurking, drawing me into lonely and weird places.

One series of brief, disorienting experiences in my junior year helped to change my attitude about my obvious bouts of OCD and bizarre religiosity. My father had me do drug deliveries for the pharmacy, and this involved hospitals, individual physicians, patients, factories, and a variety of quirky shut-in customers. But that summer he had me take drug shipments to a home for the elderly filled with psychiatric patients. When I walked down those halls I witnessed behaviors that astonished me: elderly women stripping and urging me to jump into bed with them, people with echolalia who would repeat the same phrases over and over for hours on end, and others with schizophrenia, terminal dementia, and unspeakable behaviorial problems. After seeing that scene several times, I realized that any emotional problems I might have were a mere inconvenience compared to the burden these poor souls had to endure. Those visits, and ones to the girls' criminal home, set me straight on what real problems were about. Seeing all the bizarre and terribly unhappy people there appropriately turned off any woe-is-me sensibilities. I began to appreciate the life my parents had blessed us with.

I was so busy, and my external life was so positive, I thrived throughout those years. I graduated and immediately found a college where I could continue to play football and ski against top collegiate alpine skiers in the Northeast and Canada. I entered Saint Michael's College in Vermont at seventeen. My obsessions had abated as high school progressed, but during my college freshman year I started being afflicted by other odd disorders. One day, while talking to a classmate in the cafeteria, my hands began to shake uncontrollably for no apparent reason. I was diagnosed with benign familial tremor, a genetic disorder, and still experience those shakes from time to time.

That same month, I drove back to New York to visit Diane, whom I'd been dating since high school. While driving with her that weekend I felt an unpleasant tingling in my feet that then spread up my legs to my torso. By the time this vibratory pressure wave shot into my neck, I thought the top of my head would blow off. My heart started pounding so fast that Diane freaked out because she could see my pulse in my throat and my chest was heaving violently. We pulled over and she took the wheel, picked up her mother, and drove me to the hospital. By the time I got there my blood pressure was 240 over 165, and my pulse was 142 beats per minute, a combined cardiovascular event of dangerous magnitude. The doctors pumped me with an IV solution of Valium. Within fifteen minutes my blood pressure and heart rate began to normalize.

That event would be the first of approximately 850 panic attacks I would experience over the ensuing years, mostly occurring in my twenties and early thirties, until I learned to manage them whenever I felt one coming on. But during the first five hundred panic attacks, I was certain that I was going to die within a minute or two. I would get these anytime, day or night, and it didn't matter if I was alone or in a crowd. It would just happen. It did not matter that I knew full well I would not die, having experienced these attacks before. The limbic system convinced the rest of my brain that I was about to kick the bucket. So although my OCD and episodes of dread had abated, my brain now charmed me with shaky hands and panic attacks. Nice.

One positive spin on developing panic attacks is that I was so freaked out by the potential for a stroke or heart attack that I never took hard or hallucinogenic drugs throughout college and beyond. I stuck with alcohol, and an occasional joint in certain social situations, but I do believe that, given my well-established addictions to nicotine and alcohol, the fear of losing my mind and dying of a stroke permanently kept me otherwise drug-free.

A year after the onset of the panic attacks, I was called to answer the draft for the Vietnam War. When I arranged for my physical, I was asked what conditions I had. The draft board could not have cared less about my OCD or panic attacks. But they were open to the problems my allergic asthma might present in a theater of war. So I was given an allergy scratch test on my forearm. Within ten minutes of the scratch application, I developed tunnel vision, with a dark blinding wash coming over my eyes. The next thing I knew, I was on the physician's table getting an IV. I had gone into complete anaphylactic shock from the allergens. I never received a call to the draft, and this was clearly another case where one of my inconvenient maladies probably saved my life. In fact, every one of the weird cognitive, emotional, psychiatric, and physical challenges I've been blessed with had a net positive influence on my life and my attitude toward it. Darwin would be amused.

My college years from 1965 through 1969 were probably as normal and intense and wasteful as most kids experienced in the late 1960s. I was interested in biology, skiing, and playing football. Many of my closest friends were musicians and nonscience majors, and that naturally went hand in hand with a certain level of Eastern mysticism, hallucinogens, and veritable bales of marijuana. Even snorting camphorated opiate rectal ointment was not off-limits to this confederacy, and our four-day weekend fight song, "Any Port in a Storm for a Buzz," guided those heydays of mesmerizing silliness. Just recently a former college classmate of mine, Henry (some names have been changed), reminded me of an episode that he was apparently sober enough to recall, in which I booted a guy out of a convertible and whisked away his date.

Even after college, I partied hard. In 1977, while I was a post-doctoral fellow at UC San Diego, I attended a major collegiate football game with a physician friend of mine. After the game, we headed to fraternity row, where a bunch of drunk college students in several houses thought it would be fun to move all their furniture outside. I encouraged them to pour alcohol on the furniture and light it on fire. In nearly all matters, I was both reckless and charming. When the police arrived, they didn't seem too concerned. I offered a fireman a joint, and in return he let me play with the hose, so I started spraying people. Minutes later my friend and I ran down the street to attend a large party at another fraternity house. I went up to the third floor and looked down at the band on the patio, then saw an emergency fire hose and asked the guy next to me to hand it over. I stuck it out the window and told him to turn it on. I wiped out the band, full blast. Drums were flying everywhere. A bunch of huge guys, probably football players, came up, furious, and dragged me downstairs. On my way I saw the water from the hose seeping through the ceiling of the second floor. I was put in handcuffs, and then made the cops laugh enough while convincing them that we had never really harmed anyone physically that they released me. On the run from an angry crowd, my friend and I ended up getting booted out of another frat house, then run out of an inner-city dive, and pulled over twice on the way home for suspected DUI. In all these cases I gave the police a story they enjoyed, and the two of us made it home at six a.m., just in time for him to do a twenty-four-hour ER stint and for me to start an experiment in the lab at eight a.m.

I was well out of puberty but still acting like an adolescent. And hey, a few house break-ins and, yeah, car thefts for fun really didn't mean that much back then. Boys will be boys. Most of my baby boomer friends and I feel sorry for the present Gen Y-ers who are banned from school and society for pranks we pulled on a daily basis. My early ability to make teachers and police laugh meant I never got in any real trouble. But the *Animal House* she-nanigans were clearly getting less and less controlled by the end of my adolescent years—clearly not the kind of high mark one reaches for when one has his heart and mind set on a career in the top echelon of the medical sciences. I was blowing it, but I was also having a great time.

Teenagers do dumb things, especially when they're around other teenagers and copious amounts of alcohol and drugs. I won't pretend that the antics just described betray some demon within me, waiting for any opportunity to wreak havoc on the lives of everyone I knew. But considering how calm and good-natured I was as a child, the carefree and borderline destructive attitude I adopted in college was somewhat remarkable.

At the same time I was getting myself into trouble at school, I was also adopting a laissez-faire attitude toward society at large. In the protected environs of a small Catholic school in Vermont, many of us were kept blissfully uncaring about social and political events elsewhere. We paid some homage to the imperatives of those faraway social conflicts by swearing our opposition to the Vietnam War and offering a cursory nod to the grab bag of social ills and inequities many of us were poorly equipped to understand and too distracted with partying and schoolwork to do anything about. I had been a much more sensitive humanist in high school and for the first two years of college, but those sensibilities faded as I reached twenty.

My loss of social awareness and empathy wasn't due to the environment of the college itself. Saint Michael's was founded on liberal French Enlightenment principles, which extended far beyond the classroom. The priests on the faculty were both educators and social activists and often disappeared overnight to take up the banner for whatever cause was most pressing—civil rights, Vietnam, and so on. Instead there seemed to be a crack opening and widening in my psyche, a vaguely defined door in my sensibilities that became obvious during my junior year. My behavior suggested that the change in my thinking and behavior was real, and perhaps permanent. And through that crack, on the other side of the door, was a grand hypomanic party that has never let up to this day.

My sophomore year, I enrolled in a philosophy class taught by a priest who saw something in me, something he didn't like, an emerging change of character. He wouldn't start class until I showed up and sat down, and he went so far as to hold up class one day until one of my classmates ran back to the dorm and got me out of my bed. Classmates had told him about my supposed ESP.

I never believed in it, but I would tell people what they were thinking or make predictions, probably just because I picked up on subtle physical clues, and it freaked them out. One time when I was younger, I was in my friend's backyard and pretended to be someone sitting in heaven. I named a friend of his father's and said I was driving my Jaguar XKE along Route 9E toward Lake Placid when I came around a curve and hit a tree in the road and died. Several days later that happened. My friend's father heard my prediction and said I couldn't hang out with his son anymore. People tell me I have a gift, but I say if you talk a lot you're bound to be right sometimes. In college, a few friends also said I developed a way of looking through people. Some felt scared, although they knew I wouldn't attack them. Still, it bothered them. I never tried to be a tough guy, but I was doing something that people were picking up on. The priest started calling me "evil" during class. I laughed it all off, especially since I had still not done anything I considered immoral or unethical. In my mind, my personality and character were very much intact. People said something in me was changing, something they said was rather unholy. I thought all their observations were a bunch of hooey.

As I transitioned into the upperclassman years, I renewed my interest more and more in the biological and chemical sciences, and became an even stauncher believer in the notion that behavior is all about chemistry and electricity and probably genes, and that if one could manipulate these genetic processes, one could control the brain and the mind. The film *Charly*, based on the novel *Flowers for Algernon*, came out in 1968, while I was a third-year biology student. It highlighted the biochemical basis of behaviors and resonated with me at a time when I was really receptive to it. My career as a mechanistic, reductionist, genes-control-all scientist had begun. The rest, a belief in free will and God, went missing that junior year.

Around that time, I, the former Catholic Boy of the Year in my diocese of New York, left the Catholic Church. I approached one of my professors, Father Stapleton, and told him about my doubts and asked for a formal last confession. He laughed and said, "We don't usually help people get out of the Church," but he agreed. I was still well behaved, and studious of the Scripture. I'd thoroughly learned the lessons of Christ and Aquinas and Augustine. He said, "You don't need the Church anymore, and in fact it's making you crazy, with all the OCD stuff." With that, a great dismal onus lifted, and I felt free and light. It was like a switch had flipped in my brain, one full of positive and aggressive energy, buoyed by self-confidence—maybe even overconfidence.

My belief that we are born and not made also had a profound impact on my political views. Whereas prior to college I subscribed to a mix of my mother's conservatism and my aunts' liberalism (my father was neutral), I became increasingly fed up with views on both the left and the right that environmental forces are somehow responsible for shaping who we are. For the right, this manifested itself in support of the nuclear, heterosexual family; on the left, it was rooted in the belief that society should take care of its citizens. In 1969, I became a Libertarian.

The possibilities available in a career in the neurosciences, where one deals in hard science and facts, were intoxicating to me, and I would commit my life to the study of how the brain shapes who we are. Soft psychology, although of interest to me throughout high school and the early college years, seemed to offer few real insights into what makes us human. After some temporary academic flubs and fumbles in my senior year of college, I would first teach in an all-girls Catholic high school in Albany, and then enter the physiological psychology and psychophysics graduate program at Rensselaer Polytechnic Institute in Troy. After that, I entered a doctoral program in anatomy and physiology at the University of Illinois College of Medicine in Chicago, studying, curiously enough in hindsight, the orbital cortex and temporal lobe and associated systems in the primate brain—areas I later saw damaged in killers' brains. This positioned me on a bright-line trajectory to a neurochemistry and neuroanatomy postdoctoral stint at the University of California, San Diego, before landing me a tenure-track job at the University of California, Irvine, where I have been ensconced in the ensuing years, as a satisfactorily successful professor to this day. All had been beautiful and terrifically fulfilling and easy the whole way through from college onward.

Smooth, at least, for thirty-five years.

CHAPTER 3

The Brain of a Killer

I first became interested in science when I was a child, thanks to my early experiences working on a farm, walking in the forest, and investigating life in ponds and streams in upstate New York. I was urged on in my interest of the world of bugs, frogs, and creepy crawlies by my parents and grandparents, and especially my aunt Flo, who was a nurse and graduate of Columbia University. Flo saw my interest in the natural world starting in the first years of grade school. I asked her once when she first had that insight, and she said that when I was nine months old she was bathing me in the kitchen sink, and when she drained the large porcelain basin, I had a wide-mouthed, gaping look of amazement as the water swirled down the drain. From that moment onward, she said, I was a scientist.

When we moved from Cohoes to Loudonville in 1956, Aunt Flo gave me a microbiology text from her nursing school class at Columbia, at about the same time my father gave me an old, but high-quality, vintage 1930s Bausch & Lomb microscope. I was in the fourth grade.

Oddly enough, at the same time that I developed a fascination with science and nature, I harbored my growing obsession with religion and spirituality. I began to ponder the infinite and the hereafter. Whatever had put these worries into my head, the combination of awe and fear they inspired was both thrilling and terrifying and led to a lifelong quest to understand the fundamentals of the human mind, heart, and soul.

For the first twenty years of my academic life I devoted all my work to the basic neurosciences, while also teaching medical students and graduate students about the structure and function of all the systems in the body in the gross anatomy and microanatomy courses. In the 1990s, I started teaching more and more in UCI's human neurosciences curriculum to medical students, graduate students, and residents in neurology and psychiatry, and this whetted my appetite for understanding the biological basis of the human mind, both normal and abnormal. As I became more and more knowledgeable about the human brain, as opposed to just animal brain neuroanatomy, I was being asked by more and more colleagues in psychiatry and in the behavioral and cognitive sciences to analyze brain scans of their patients in the clinical trials they were conducting for drug companies. I was developing a reputation for knowing about the entire brain and nervous system, and this lack of specialization fit my childhood dream of becoming a Renaissance man, like my hero, Leonardo da Vinci. So instead of becoming an expert in something, I was actually becoming an expert in nothing at all.

One day in 1995, my colleague in psychiatry Anthony rang me up and said, "Hey, Jim, I've got a job for you. These lawyers I'm consulting have a guy who murdered some people, and we did a scan to see if there was something wrong with his brain. Could you take a look and tell us what you see?" I said sure and reviewed his PET scan.

A PET (positron emission tomography) scan is a tool used in radiology to determine the functioning of the body, specifically small areas the size of a grain of sand in tissues and organs. It is particularly useful in looking into organs, such as the brain, that are encased in bone. The PET scan is considered a functional rather than merely structural scan because it measures the functioning of the brain. Radioactive molecules that interact with the brain in specific ways are injected before the scan. They can be sugars, to measure the brain's metabolism, or drugs that link to the receptors for various neurotransmitters, to measure the distribution of those receptors.

In this scan the doctors used an isotope of fluorine, F-18, bound to a type of glucose taken up by active brain cells. It remains in the cells and emits positrons, a form of radiation, for about an hour. The glucose is injected into a vein in the subject's arm, and then the subject is slid onto a gurney into the PET scanner until the head is surrounded by the detectors. The amount of time the "photograph" of the brain is taken depends on the half-life of the isotope. In the case of F-18 this exposure time is thirty minutes, so the image that is obtained is a snapshot of brain activity that occurs in this thirty-minute period. During this time, the F-18 releases positrons that immediately collide with electrons, resulting in a release of energy detected in the coils surrounding the head in the PET scanner. The scanner's computer software

locates the source of all of the collisions, and is then able to recon-
struct a 3-D image of them in the entire brain. We assign colors
to the density of collisions, indicating use of glucose, and thus
brain activity. The darker the area, the harder that part of the
brain is working.

So I looked at the scan and saw, compared to a healthy brain,
a decrease of activity in the orbital cortex and the area around the
amygdala. In a healthy brain, this area prevents impulsivity (i.e.,
it inhibits behavior), so when it is turned off, the person is impulsive. I relayed this to my colleague. The sicko's lawyers then told
the judge that as a matter of biology, their client couldn't control
himself, and he received life without parole instead of the death
penalty. Anthony spread the word and I got more calls like this,
analyzing the brains of about fifteen psychopathic killers over the
next decade—many of them famous. I can't reveal any details for
legal reasons, but it was clear from their actions that they were not
just impulsive killers but real methodical psychos.

Today people ask me why I didn't drop everything and pursue
research on psychopathy, but I had a lot of other things going on.
Collaborations with my clinical colleagues grew in scope in the
early 1990s, and then they began to dominate my research interests by 2000, along with my studies of adult stem cells. Eventually
this interest and involvement with human psychiatric studies led
me to move my academic appointment to the Department of Psychiatry and Human Behavior. Based on these studies, starting in
the early and mid-1990s, I started to give more and more scientific, and then public and lay, talks on personality, development,

schizophrenia, addictions, male-female brain differences, emotional memory, and consciousness. By 1998, I was giving a mix of talks about stem cells and psychiatric research, and in 2000, our lab made a breakthrough discovery regarding how adult stem cells mobilize to repair brain injuries. The study was sent from the National Institutes of Health to the U.S. Congress as the first evidence that adult stem cells, as opposed to just embryonic stem cells, could be mobilized in the damaged adult brain, perhaps to cure Parkinson's disease, stroke, and other neurodegenerative disorders. The work surrounding this finding diverted much of my energy and focus for the better part of six years starting in 2001. Meanwhile, our lab received three large federal grants, one to study the nature of tobacco addiction and two to design computing systems for medical imaging. I was also starting a biotech company, NeuroRepair. So for the entire time leading up to discovering my own abnormal brain scan and what it might mean, I rarely thought of psychopaths.

In 2005, I was contacted by the psychiatrist Daniel Amen, who uses brain imaging to study psychiatric disorders such as ADHD, PTSD, and Alzheimer's. From his expert testimony work over the years Amen had amassed about fifty brain scans of murderers, both psychopathic and impulsive, and he was curious whether I might find a pattern in them. I told him to send them over, but to take off the tags and mix them with other scans—those of healthy subjects, people with schizophrenia, and people with depression.

I did the analysis in a blind process, something we always try to do in science and especially where perceived patterns in data are so easily influenced by prior knowledge and bias toward the subject. When I considered all of the brains, the underlying brain circuitry patterns I saw fell into easily discernible groups—including two different types of killers. From the moment when the blind codes were all broken and I saw who was who in the groups, I became transfixed by what the information might portend.

To better understand exactly what I saw in these scans and why it was so relevant, you first need to have a basic understanding of the human brain. The brain is organized in a bewildering number of ways, even to a silverback neuroscientist. The researcher Floyd Bloom once called it an "electrified jelly," which is certainly what it seems like to a first-year medical student.

Neuroanatomists categorize themselves into "clumpers" and "splitters" based on how they like to organize the brain. Clumpers prefer to simplify the brain into as few sections as possible, while splitters divide the brain into thousands of pieces, all with their own Latin or Greek names. To make things even more confusing, splitters like to throw into the mix the name of the scientist who first described that brain area, so we end up with names like "Zuckerkandl's fasciculus," "the ventral tegmental relay zone of Giolli," and the "nucleus reticularis tegmenti pontis of Bechterew." This is one of the reasons medical students are terrified of their first course in neuroscience.

When these brain areas, their connections, chemistry, and circuitry, are considered together for any adaptive behavior, for example an infant expressing fear at the sight of a stranger, the complexity of the brain's wiring can start to get out of hand. For clinical sciences the representation of the relevant wiring of the brain can quickly send one packing to the nearest pub for a cold one. For example, here is a "simplified" version of the brain circuitry involved in depression. Don't let this figure put you off. Everyone, including neuroscientists, hates these kinds of figures of the brain, but the brain is extraordinarily complex, so we have to deal with these Jackson Pollock monstrosities from time to time.

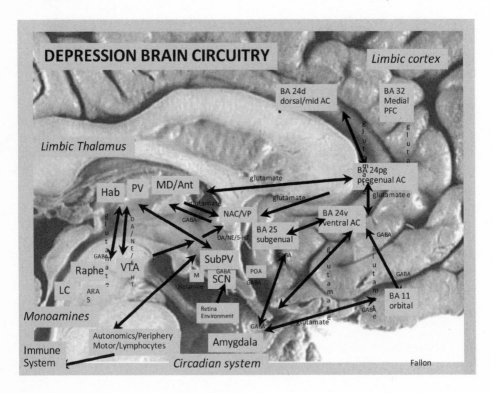

FIGURE 3A: Depression brain circuitry.

Most of us, however, fall somewhere in between these camps and organize the brain into a few hundred parts. I am a splitter, and I like having thousands of specific parts to study. But for the sake of simplicity, especially when teaching or writing a paper, I like to organize the brain into a 3×3×3 "Rubik's Cube" pattern. This twenty-seven-part brain is as simple as I'm willing to go and still be able to sleep at night without violating Einstein's first law of simplicity in science: "Everything should be made as simple as possible, but not simpler."

Everyone is familiar with the idea that we have a left brain and a right brain. But this conception is woefully lacking in some important ways. On the next page is a drawing of the side of the brain at the top left, a view of the top of the brain looking down from above, and a view of the medial portion of the brain that you would see if you sliced the brain down the middle. This medial piece between the left and right hemispheres is also called the limbic lobe, from the word *limbus*, which means "edge" in Latin, and here refers to a full circle of ancient cortex related to emotion, attention, memory, switching between cognitive and emotional states, and even helping you to see if someone has taken one of your french fries when you weren't looking.

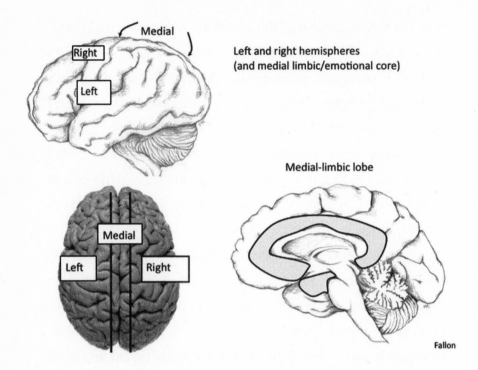

FIGURE 3B: Brain hemispheres.

The next slicing of the Rubik's Cube brain is from front, or anterior, to back, or posterior. The most posterior region of the cortex is dedicated to the visual sensory system, as well as "association" cortices that have functions more complicated than simple seeing or touching or hearing, but rather cognitive tasks such as spatial processing. The external world—up, down, left, right, close up, far away—is mapped onto the cortex in the upper part of the posterior area, called the superior parietal cortex. People with damage to this brain area on one side will ignore the other half of their sensory world. So they may only perceive the numbers on the left side of a clock dial, but not the right side. Given a blank circle, they will fill in the numbers on the dial from 1 to 12, but these will all be drawn on just one half of the clock. If the damage is done to the hemisphere that controls their nondominant hand, let's say the right superior parietal cortex for a right-hander (each hemisphere controls the opposite side of the body), then they will go the extra step in their "agnosia." They will be able to move the opposite leg, and feel a pinch on that leg, but they may ask the doctor or nurse to remove the leg from the hospital bed because it is foreign and doesn't belong to their body.

Another function of this posterior area is the understanding and conceptual creation of language. In the dominant hemisphere (the left side if you're right-handed), this language function enables us to master syntax and grammar, while in the nondominant hemisphere, this language function allows us to understand the song and rhythm of language, as well as humor. It appears that the dominant hemisphere function is more genetically determined, while the nondominant hemisphere function is more molded by environment. That is, you will learn to mirror the accents and cadence and patois of speech from your family and friends, but your basic ability for grammar and syntax is more genetically determined. One tends to adopt the song and rhythm of speech around the time one reaches puberty, but the range and capabilities of individuals vary widely. In the case of Henry Kissinger and his younger brother, Walter, who fled Nazi Germany in 1938, when Henry was sixteen and his brother was fourteen, the elder brother kept his pronounced Frankish accent while Walter sounded very American.

In the Rubik's Cube middle sector of the hemisphere, there are the somatic and motor areas that map the skin senses in the back half of this middle piece, and the map of the areas that control the muscles of the body. Just in front of this motor cortex is the premotor cortex, which is involved in the planning of motor movements and in learning the rules of how we swing a golf club and play the piano. These two motor-related cortices form a strip on each hemisphere in size and placement like the support arms of a set of earphones.

The anterior, or front, section is the prefrontal cortex and is responsible for the so-called executive functions of the brain, including knowing rules, making plans, and enabling short-term memory. This "scratch pad" memory lasts seconds or tens of seconds and helps us to remember phone numbers long enough to dial them and tells us, without looking, where we set our drink while we're eating or playing poker. The prefrontal cortex is the brain region most important for the elaboration of personality and character, and the control of impulse, obsessions, and antisocial behavior.

Besides being the locus of will, the prefrontal cortex is related to a myriad of functions we consider particularly well developed in primates, especially humans. These involve what has been called "memory of the future," that is, projecting one's mind into the future to imagine, or experience, really, how one will remember an act that has not yet taken place. This is akin to the pleasant sensation one has when playing a game of chess and knowing that after just five moves one will cream his opponent. This knowledge of the imagined future resides in a circuit centered in the prefrontal cortex.

I suspect that humans' ability to do this relies, in part, on a mutation in the gene for catechol-O-methyltransferase, or COMT. This enzyme is responsible for breaking down dopamine in the frontal lobe after it has been released. There are two possible versions of the mutation, which, taken together, are referred to as the valine-methionine polymorphism. The methionine version of the gene leads to the production of a COMT enzyme that has a lower melting point, while the valine version codes for a COMT with a higher melting point. All this means is that, in those with the methionine version, COMT inactivates faster at normal brain temperature, allowing dopamine to hang around synapses triggering neuronal function for a longer period of time, since there is no enzyme to break down the neurotransmitter. The steady supply of dopamine enhances frontal lobe activity, including its capacities to brainstorm and premeditate. Thanks to this and other neurotransmitter-related mutations millions of years ago, early humans could plan further ahead and anticipate future events like war and famine. And because they could anticipate these events, they did things like invent weapons and learn to farm. Likewise, memory of the future allows us to appreciate a sense of time and helps explain our belief in religion, the afterlife, and eternity.

The next way we can slice the brain's hemispheres is into upper, middle, and lower thirds, more correctly referred to as the dorsal, intermediate, and ventral streams.

The upper, or dorsal, stream lies right under where you wear a ten-gallon hat. This "stream," so called by Leslie Ungerleider of the National Institute of Mental Health, is primarily concerned with processing "where" things are in your external environment, as well as their movements. The lower, or ventral, stream processes "what" things are in your external world, especially in the visual system. The intermediate stream codes for "when" things happen, but is also involved intimately with language and the mirror neuron system (explained in chapter 7).

The dorsal part of the prefrontal cortex and its interconnecting subcortical areas are associated with "cold cognition," emotionless processing of thoughts, perceptions, short-term or executive memories, plans, and rule-making. This involves both generating these thoughts and also inhibiting other thoughts, depending on established rules for success and failure in the appropriate context. Life is full of rules and contingencies, whether in Scrabble or golf or business, and the dorsal prefrontal cortex tells you when it's okay to act on your urges—when you should place a tile or hit a ball or buy a stock—and when you shouldn't. The lower, or ventral, part of the prefrontal cortex, largely made up of the orbital cortex and ventromedial prefrontal cortex, is involved in similar functions, but more those enabling and disenabling "hot cognition"—emotional memory and socially, ethically, and morally programmed behaviors. Someone with a highly functioning dorsal prefrontal system would have superior planning and executive functions, whereas someone with a highly functioning ventral prefrontal system would have superior control over impulsive and inappropriate interpersonal and social behaviors. Likewise, lower functioning in these systems leads to not only a lack of comprehension of these high-order behaviors, but an inability to control them under socially inappropriate circumstances.

Connecting with others involves both cold (rational) cognition, where one person understands what others might be thinking and what an appropriate response might be, and hot (emotional) cognition, where one can experience empathy with another's feelings and attitudes—that is, actually "feel" them much like the other person would experience them. Someone with damage to the hot system, let's say in the orbital cortex, might not be able to predict others' thoughts but will have the most trouble sharing his feelings. A dichotomy may exist between empathy, a fundamental connection with the pain of others and arising very early in life, and "theory of mind," a more elaborated medial prefrontal system that allows us to consider others' thoughts and beliefs, even if they're different from our own. People with autism lack theory of mind but not empathy, while people with psychopathy lack empathy but not theory of mind. Without empathy you can still have sympathy, though—the ability to retrieve emotional memories, including those that can predict what painful event is probably about to befall another person, and the will to help that person.

These brain circuits mature at different times during development, and although there are major maturational events that take place in the terrible twos, puberty, late adolescence, the twenties, and the mid-thirties, some are not completely integrated until one is in the sixties, which appears to be the typical average peak time of human insight, cognition, and understanding in many realms of life.

The central cube in the Rubik's Cube brain consists of the subcortical structures that lie deep in the cortex, and these include the basal ganglia, the thalamus, and the brain stem. The basal ganglia are a region important for understanding how cognition and emotion interact to facilitate or turn off behavior. It is a yin-yang area in dynamic balance where dopamine and the endorphins may have opposite effects on adjacent neurons, and where motivation, drive, hedonism, addictions, sensory-motor activity, and all sorts of fascinating behaviors get their oomph.

There are millions of so-called loops of neuronal connections that pass through the basal ganglia, integrating cortical command information with other subcortical way stations such as the thalamic structures (called the thalamus, epithalamus, subthalamus, and hypothalamus), brain stem, and cerebellar circuits.

Some of these loops are closed, or direct, feedback loops connecting the same brain areas over and over, while others are open loops where the information is passed to adjacent brain channels for integrating, say, different modalities of perception, emotion, consciousness, attention, planning, and will.

Within each loop there are parallel channels, one of which leads to motor action and is thus a "Do It" channel, and its partner, which keeps you from doing something, and is thus a "Don't Do It" channel. These two converge on motor neurons that add up the "Do Its" (excitation) and the "Don't Do Its" (inhibition) and determine whether you move. Since dopamine turns *on* the "Do It" channel, and simultaneously turns *off* the "Don't Do It" channel in the loops, dopamine is the key neurotransmitter that flips the switch when you are lying on your couch watching the game and decide you want to go get a beer. People whose dopamine cells die do not have this ability to get up from the couch. These people have Parkinson's disease. They have the will to get up (prefrontal cortex), and they have the plan (premotor cortex) and command signal (motor cortex) to get up and start walking, but they don't have the dopamine to activate and deactivate these "Do It" and "Don't Do It" channels to get the movement started.

There are millions of these closed and open loops in the brain connecting the cortex and subcortical areas, and in this way broad areas of the brain become involved in even the seemingly simplest of behaviors we take for granted. This is why when we look at a PET scan or fMRI scan or EEG, just a finger tap can activate many brain areas in both cortical and subcortical areas.

As I looked at the scans of killers Amen sent, there were a few features I expected to see in the psychopaths. They would have decreased activity in the orbital cortex—the part of the prefrontal cortex just above the orbits, or eye sockets—and the nearby ventromedial prefrontal cortex. These are involved in inhibition, social behavior, ethics, and morality. I expected psychopaths would also have damage to the front of the temporal lobe, including the amygdala, which processes emotions, leading to cold behavior. I'd seen these neural deficits in other scans of psychopathic killers, and they'd also been identified in more formal research by other labs.

So I pointed to the scans I thought belonged to the psychopathic killers. When we looked up their code numbers, I'd nailed it. When a neuroanatomist sees a pattern, he goes crazy. I could have been studying butterflies and I still would have gotten excited. Patterns are where we get our buzz. And that's when I really became interested in psychopathy.

Combining these scans with others of diagnosed psychopaths I'd collected over the years, I noticed a more intricate pattern. In psychopaths, I saw a loss of activity that extends from the orbital cortex into the ventromedial prefrontal cortex and into a part of the prefrontal cortex called the anterior cingulate. The loss then continues along the cingulate cortex to the back of the brain as a thin strip, then loops down into the lower part of the temporal lobe into the very tip of the temporal lobe and the amygdala.

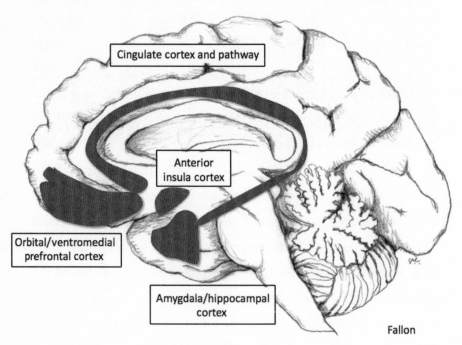

FIGURE 3C: Brain areas dysfunctional in psychopaths.

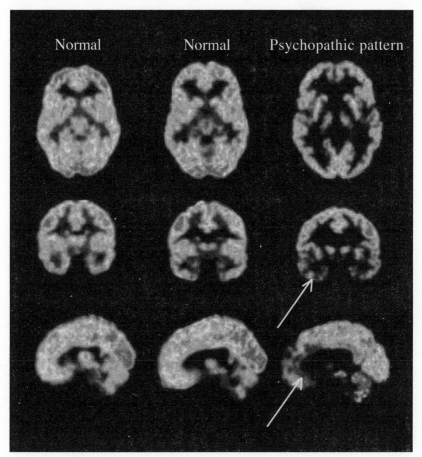

FIGURE 3D: PET scans of normal brains and that of a psychopath.

All of these areas of loss make up the major chunk of brain called the limbic, or emotional, cortex, since this is the main area regulating emotion. This loop of loss of cortical function comes full circle, as I noticed that the "connector" strip of cortex between the orbital, cingulate, and temporal cortex—the insula—also showed signs of damage or low function in these psychopathic killers. In previous studies of psychopaths' brains, most attention had been on the orbital and ventromedial prefrontal cortex and the amygdala. I filled in the picture, identifying other areas related to anxiety and empathy, and explaining how psychopaths could sometimes remain so cool and collected. The simplicity and elegance of this pattern exhilarated me as I felt I had perhaps discovered a sliver of the Holy Grail for understanding awful, predatory human behavior.

I wondered how the functioning of the frontal lobe, specifically the lower (ventral) and medial (along the midline) portions of the prefrontal cortex, would lead to some of the traits generally seen in psychopathy. A psychopath has a poorly functioning ventral system, usually used for hot cognition, but he can have a normal or even supernormal dorsal system, so that without the bother of conscience and empathy, the cold planning and execution of predatory behaviors becomes finely tuned, convincing, highly manipulative, and formidable. Because psychopaths' dorsal systems work so well, they can learn how to appear that they care, thus making them even more dangerous.

The other brain areas related to psychopathologies are the amygdala in the anterior inner region of the temporal lobe, the hidden insula, bridging the orbital cortex and anterior temporal lobe, and the cingulate and parahippocampal cortices, also connecting the prefrontal cortex and amygdala in a looping fashion. These areas of the brain of the psychopath were later shown in a thorough and well-done series of MRI studies in 2011 and 2012 by Kent Kiehl's research group at the MIND Institute at the University of New Mexico.

As discussed before, all of these are lumped together as the limbic cortex, or cortices associated with the processing and elaboration of emotion. These areas are critical to understanding the psychopathic brain, for these, as well as the orbital and ventromedial prefrontal cortices, are maldeveloped or have sustained early damage. This finding was not a surprise to me, as all these brain areas had been implicated in individual syndromes related to lack of inhibition, sexual hyperfunction, and problems with moral reasoning. What was surprising was that psychopaths all showed these brain areas with lower activity, while other types of criminals, for example impulsive murderers, had a different pattern where one of these areas would show lower function, but not all the areas together.

For example, in impulsive people there is often a malfunctioning of the orbital cortex, and in hypersexual and rage-prone people there is often amygdaloid dysfunction. In people with parahippocampal and amygdala damage, one often finds inadequacies in emotional memory, sexuality, and social behavior, and in people with cingulate dysfunction, there can be problems with mood regulation and behavioral control. But the pattern of decreased functioning across the entire complex of these limbic, prefrontal, and temporal cortices—whether due to prenatal development, perinatal maternal stress, substance abuse, direct trauma, or a severe rare combination of "high-risk" genes—appeared unique to the psychopath's brain.

No one had reported on the combination of prefrontal and temporal lobe underfunction, I noticed, and this motivated me to try my theory out on professional audiences, even though I was not an expert in the area at that time. It was a new field and no one had established expertise. But given my neuroanatomical background, I was trained to visualize and explain previously unknown brain circuits in the normal and abnormal brain. I began giving talks on the subject in 2005 to several medical research universities and law schools in the United States, Europe, and Israel, and to the National Science Foundation Mathematical Biosciences Institute. I also gave one to the Moritz College of Law, after which they invited me to write my first paper on violent psychopaths—the one I was working on the day I discovered my own scan. I wanted to organize my own thoughts on what makes these nasty fellows tick—and then explode into the worst kinds of violence.

In 2005, I was also doing multiple studies on Alzheimer's disease. For one study, I needed to analyze a number of healthy comparison subjects. I figured we might as well look at a whole family, for an added dimension. So I scanned the brains of my mother, my aunt, three of my brothers, Diane, me, and our three kids. Fortunately everyone turned out fine. At least on the Alzheimer's front.

This was when the realization mentioned at the beginning of this book occurred. Looking at my family's scans, I saw one that I thought had been mixed in from the psychopathic killers' scans. It turned out to be my own. I had the trademark inactivity in the orbital, ventral, and temporal cortices as well as connecting tissue.

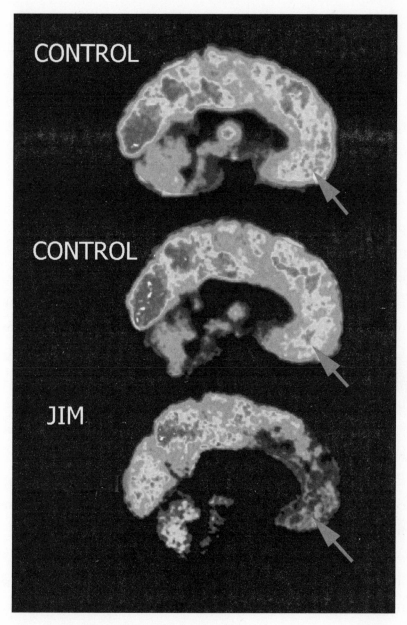

FIGURE 3E: My PET scan (with two controls).

My first reaction: "You've got to be kidding me." It blew me away. Then I just laughed. I said to myself, "Oh, I get the joke." If you were asked over the years to look at killers' brains and found a pattern to them, and then found out you had the same pattern, that's funny. If I'd thought for a moment that I really was a psychopath, I may have reacted more soberly. But I didn't.

One reason for my denial was that, despite my research into the brain and behavior, I had very little understanding of what a psychopath was, since psychopaths weren't the focus of my lab. In my mind, they were mostly violent, unstable individuals who lacked empathy and thrived on manipulation. Love me or hate me, I was not a criminal. My brain may have looked a lot like those of the murderers I'd been studying, but I had never killed or ruthlessly assaulted anyone. I had never fantasized about committing violence or doing harm to another individual. I was a successful, happily married father of three—a pretty normal guy.

Most of my colleagues wouldn't find out about my scan for three more years, but I mentioned it in a few of my talks on psychopathy. People said, "That's pretty wild, but what does it mean?" They couldn't process it. I obviously was not a psychopathic killer like the people I'd been studying, so no one made a big deal out of it.

I mentioned the scan to my family, but they're not scientists. They just said, "Oh, interesting." Diane told me, "I've known you my whole life, and you've never hit me. That scan is curious, but the proof is in the pudding. Sure, you've got a lot of bad behaviors, but you're not that."

And I didn't question her.

CHAPTER 4

Bloodlines

Although I wasn't worried I was a psychopath, the revelation that my own scan fit perfectly with the pattern of the scans of the psychopathic killers did give me reason to pause. I'd been so sure I'd discovered something profound that would help us better understand what makes a psychopath a psychopath, but the disconnect between my brain pattern and my behavior might imply that my theory of the psychopath brain was wrong, or, at the very least, incomplete.

In December 2005, two months after I discovered my abnormal brain scans, my wife, Diane, and I hosted a barbecue for our immediate family one Sunday in our backyard. As I was grilling various meats and veggies, my mother, Jennie, pulled me aside. "I hear you've been going around the country talking about murderers' brains," she whispered. She knew I'd given a few lectures in which I mentioned that my own brain looked just like a killer's. "I think there is something you should look at."

She had my full attention.

"Your cousin Dave mentioned a new historical book that was published, and it is about our family. Well, actually, it's about your father's family." My cousin David Bohrer, a no-frills, intellectual, and nimble-witted newspaper editor, is an avid family genealogy buff and came across this book in his research. He and I had discussed family history for years, and he had mentioned the book to me without any particular value-added heads-up concerning what it was about. I had ordered it a few months before but hadn't bothered to read it.

"I know about the book, Ma, but haven't had time to read it yet."

"Why not?"

"Please, Mums, I'll look at it after dinner."

I knew the bum's rush I was giving my mother wasn't going to keep her at bay for long. As a teenager, she had successfully broken through the otherwise impenetrable defenses of Elsa Einstein, wife of Albert, after seeing her on the streets of Poughkeepsie, to gain favor for her husband's autograph. Sixty years later I had lost her in a crowd outside the Los Angeles County Museum of Art, only to track her down fifteen minutes later duking it out with radio rock jock Rick Dees—she thought modern-day music was much too loud and the lyrics disgraceful and wanted to tell him about it. I had also seen her lecture our family friend George Carlin several times about the use of profanity in his acts; he was, after all, plenty funny enough without having to resort to such cheap and vulgar word games, Jennie said. This diminutive Sicilian, who was still, at eighty-nine, a sharp-tongued *principessa*, would not be easily put off by her son's disinterest in her book recommendation. But, out of respect for the time-honored rule that a meal cooked properly comes first, she relented.

A half hour after finishing dinner I stole away to my office for a bit and sat down to a double espresso and a glass of black anisette, with the obligatory thirteen coffee beans thrown in. As I munched on the beans and sipped the coffee and liqueur, I skimmed the book. It was called *Killed Strangely: The Death of Rebecca Cornell*, by Elaine Forman Crane, and it detailed the murder of seventy-three-year-old Rebecca Cornell by her forty-six-year-old son, Thomas, in 1673. This was one of the first cases of matricide in the American colonies. (The Cornell family tree is of some general interest to an American history buff, as Rebecca is an ancestor of Ezra Cornell, the founder and namesake of Cornell University.)

Rebecca lived in a large house on a one-hundred-acre plot along the Narragansett Bay in Rhode Island with Thomas and his family. One night after dinner she was found charred and smoldering near the fireplace in her bedroom, almost unrecognizable. Originally the death was decreed an "Unhappie Accident," but Rebecca's brother was soon visited by an apparition suggesting foul play. Thomas, financially dependent on his mother, had not always gotten along with her and was at times abusive. Rebecca's body was exhumed for a closer examination, and a suspicious wound was found in her stomach, the result of a possible stabbing. Despite weak evidence, Thomas was convicted and hanged.

My mother wasn't just interested in Rebecca's story because she had warped taste in entertainment. According to David, Rebecca Cornell was our great-great-great-great-great-great-great-great-great grandmother in our patrilineal line. And it turned out that Thomas wasn't the only murderer in the Cornell clan. Rebecca, the book pointed out, was also a direct ancestor of Lizzie Borden, the putative ax murderer accused of killing her father and stepmother in 1892. That made Borden, according to David, our cousin. The book reported that between 1673 and 1892, there would be a handful of other murderers and suspected murderers in our patrilineal line, each one of whom had been accused or convicted of killing a close family member. Rebecca's descendant Alvin Cornell murdered his wife, Hannah, in 1843, using first an iron shovel handle to strike her, then a razor to slit her throat. The Cornells' penchant for killing their own, I mused, was damned civic-minded of our lot, and happily, and somewhat conclusively, the trail seems to have run cold at the end of the nineteenth century, making me and my father several generations removed from *that* side of the family.

David and our other cousin Arnold Fallon have researched our family tree with great energy and expertise. Through their tireless genealogical efforts, including visits to cemeteries scattered throughout New England, New York, Kansas, and California, they continue to discover new and juicy family tidbits. In 2011 and 2012, they found two other paternal lines of grandfathers where further mayhem is still being uncovered, including one line of suspected and convicted murderers (for a total of seven in the family, two of them women), and one line of grandfathers with a penchant for leaving their wives and families for either other women or completely unknown reasons. In both of these lineages, and the Cornell line, our male ancestors were unkind or downright homicidal to people in their immediate families only, never to strangers.

Going further back, my distant grandfather King John Lackland (1167–1216) is known as the most brutal, and hated, of the English monarchs, in spite of the fact that he signed one of the most important antimonarchical documents of all time, the Magna Carta. John was quite the all-pro prick, said to have lacked scruples (something a close friend once said about me), been treacherous, and to have a "puckish" sense of humor (something my uncle Bob once said of me). He had very high energy—hypomania if not mania—and was highly distrustful, unstable, cruel, and ruthless. A near-contemporary of his said, "John was a tyrant. He was a wicked ruler who did not behave like a king. He was greedy and took as much money as he could from his people. Hell is too good for a horrible person like him." But kind things, almost, have been said about him, too. In *King John: England's Evil King?*, the historian Ralph Turner wrote, "John had potential for great success. He had intelligence, administrative ability and he was good at planning military campaigns. However, too many personality flaws held him back."

John's father, Grandpa King Henry II (1154–1189), was like John in that he also went into violent rages. At times they got so pissed off that they foamed at the mouth. Henry was killed by his son. Grandpa Henry III and Grandpa Edward I, like King John, were also known to be a bit aggressive, impulsive, and mean-spirited, and all four were brutal toward Jews. Henry III made Jews wear a badge of shame in public, and Edward I expelled the Jews from England in 1290, but not before executing three hundred of them. Edward was feared one-on-one. He was big, powerful, and aggressive and was referred to as a leopard (in a derogatory way) in "The Song of Lewes" in 1264. The historian Michael Prestwich wrote that the dean of St. Paul's confronted Edward over taxation and died (somehow) on the spot at the king's feet, so he may have been murdered by hand, although I have never seen that confirmed.

Diane and I visited a "family" castle (Caerphilly Castle) in Wales in 2004. This was the roost of Grandfather Gilbert de Clare. He also massacred Jews (1264) at Canterbury. Another bad guy in this same line is John Fitzalan. In one campaign he rested up in a nunnery, where his men (and he?) raped all the women inside, then ransacked the neighborhood in Brittany. Right after this, on his boat just off the coast, some of his men became frightened of a storm, so he murdered them. This is only a sampling, but suffice it to say I do not come from a line of mensches.

I knew my mother was pleased by these developments. Jennie, whose full Sicilian name is Giovannina Giuseppina Salvetrica Sylvia Scoma, is the daughter of Sicilian immigrants who, like many others who had come to America to make their way up in the world, had engaged in some dubious activities over the course of their lives. My grandfather Tomas held various respectable jobs while my mother and her siblings grew up: court interpreter, barber, pinsetter, musician—but even after he moved the family from Brooklyn, where my mother was born, to Poughkeepsie, he worked each week in Brooklyn running numbers—that is, orchestrating an illicit lottery—and selling enough bootleg merchandise to open his own restaurant. This being the Prohibition era, my mother and her brother and three sisters supported their father's entrepreneurial endeavor by bootlegging beer. My father and his family, unsuspecting of their own unsavory roots, loved to tease my mother about her past. So I wasn't surprised to notice a devilish twinkle in Jennie's eyes as she told me about my father's bloodthirsty ancestors.

As with my brain scan, the discovery of this book—and, later, the rest of the history—didn't trouble me too much. To me, it was the sort of revelation one might even brag about, akin to discovering your family is made up of more horse thieves than blue bloods.

I also knew that ancestry is not genetics, and, given the amount of dilution of genetic impact at each mixing generation, it is hard to make a case that such a long and checkered lineage over centuries would determine why and how a particular person would behave, and misbehave. Nonetheless, in our family we know of at least two lines of killers and one line of wife abandoners. This type of genetic parlor game makes one wonder whether a slight tendency for some traits might percolate through so many generations to the present. Complicating the story, my father, my grandfather Harry Cornell Fallon, and two uncles who fought in World War II were conscientious objectors, but nonetheless were medics in battles at Iwo Jima, New Guinea, and New Caledonia. I should point out, however, that my grandfather loved to brawl. Also, in my own generation of brothers and cousins, at least five are aggressive and fearless boxers and street fighters. They actually *like* to fight, and will even take on several people at a time by themselves. These hombres are fearless and aggressive. But they are also great partyers, funny, and smart.

My family history would take on a new level of gravitas when I started to learn about my own genes. As part of the Alzheimer's brain scan study, my lab had taken blood samples for genetic analysis. And as soon as I saw my own scan, I decided we should check those samples for aggression-related traits.

How do genes affect behavior? To begin to answer this question, it's important to understand some basics about genetics.

There are approximately twenty thousand genes in the human genome. The genes are located in forty-six chromosomes (twenty-three pairs), one set in the pairs derived from the mother, one set from the father, in the nucleus of most cells of the body. The only cells that don't contain all forty-six chromosomes are the germ cells in the testes or ovaries, each of which has twenty-three chromosomes, or half the number in the somatic cells. Cells that contain all forty-six chromosomes are called diploid cells since they contain both pairs, while germ cells are called haploid.

Chromosomes are composed of DNA, the master blueprint of a cell. DNA is coded on the sequence of four different chemicals called bases. The bases sit in pairs with T (thymine) coupled with

A (adenine) and G (guanine) coupled with C (cytosine). The forty-six-chromosome (diploid) genome contains over six billion base pairs. Sequences of base pairs, called genes, code for and produce gene products such as proteins. If just one of the base pairs is altered by mutation, say from ultraviolet damage, a virus, or cigarette smoke, the resulting protein will be aberrant, and usually faulty.

Some of these mutations are not fatal and are actually kept by the cells and the population. These are called single nucleotide polymorphisms, or SNPs. If the incidence of the change is found in less than 1 percent of the population of humans, it is called a mutation; if more than 1 percent, it is typically called an SNP. There are about twenty million SNPs found in humans, and they account for many differences in the appearance and behavior of people, from curly hair to obesity to drug addiction. It is these SNPs where the hunt for genetic "causes" of traits and diseases has focused since the 1990s.

Other important alterations to the genetic code involve so-called promoters and inhibitors, pieces of genes that regulate the gene's ability to make products. Some of these products regulate the behavior of neurotransmitters. So promoters and inhibitors are like the gas and brake pedals of a gene as they control the delivery of neurotransmitters like serotonin and dopamine in the brain. For serotonin, implicated in depression, bipolar disorder, sleep and eating disorders, schizophrenia, hallucinations and panic attacks, as well as psychopathy, the breakdown enzyme is MAO-A. MAOA, the gene that produces this enzyme (and lacks its hyphen), has a promoter that comes in either a short form or a long form. The version of the MAOA gene with the short promoter has been associated with aggressive behavior and is called the "warrior gene."

There are probably twenty to fifty or more SNPs involved in causing most diseases. Therefore, statements that the warrior gene "causes" aggression, violence, and retaliation raises the hackles of geneticists, since there are probably dozens or more "warrior genes" in people who are particularly violent. But even the simple diseases (called Mendelian diseases, after the godfather of genetics, Gregor Mendel)—like cystic fibrosis, which is caused by a single mutation in the gene that codes for the chloride channel in cell membranes regulating water balance in the lungs and gut and glands—can appear as fifty different disorders in fifty different individuals with the disease. In the case of cystic fibrosis, that single chloride channel mutation affects other cellular and organ components. The gene-gene interaction, or more correctly gene product–gene product interaction, is called epistasis, and this effect must also be considered when determining the causes, symptoms, and cures for diseases of all kinds, even psychiatric disorders.

The neurotransmitter dopamine is implicated in several psychiatric disorders. Drugs that increase dopamine transmission can alleviate symptoms of depression, and drugs that reduce it can alleviate schizophrenia. The impetus to initiate a behavior "considered" by the prefrontal cortex is largely under the energetic control of dopamine, which is mostly produced in the midbrain.

When dopamine is released, things happen. Dopamine doesn't decide exactly *what* will happen, but how quickly and strongly something happens, and for how long, much like an accelerator pedal on a car.

How much the monoamines such as serotonin and dopamine affect each person depends on the person's genetic makeup and the maturity of the underlying circuitry—especially for the genes that control the synthesis of these neurotransmitters—but much more importantly on the enzymes, such as MAO-A, that break them down and terminate their synaptic action. Also of significance are the levels of synthesis and activity of the receptors for these monoamines, which number in the dozens, as well as the genes controlling the efficacy of synaptic membrane protein transporters, which pull neurotransmitters out of the synapses, or spaces between cells, and stop their signaling. These transporters are implicated in some pretty exotic brain functions, for example creative dance performance and a sense of spirituality. It is apparent that with all the possible allelic combinations of monoamine-relevant genes, as well as glutamate, the amino acid gamma amino butyric acid (GABA), and cholinergic systems in these cortices, there are thousands of kinds of "normal" prefrontal cortices. These thousands of types of prefrontal cortices can possess different amounts of highly variable traits such as memory, emotionality, aggressiveness, and sexuality. Likewise, because of all the genetic variables, there are really a limitless number of ways to be schizophrenic or depressed. Some prefrontal disorders are more complex than others, and certainly schizophrenia is one of the most complex. But there are also probably many ways to be a psychopath, too, considering all of the combined neural systems and genetic factors involved. Unfortunately, very little is known of the biological basis, especially genetics, of the brains of psychopaths.

Despite the impressive numbers associated with the human genome, the information carried on those twenty thousand genes, forty-six chromosomes, and six billion base pairs tells only 5 percent of the story. The remaining 95 percent resides in a still-mysterious garnish of noncoding nucleic acids, bits of DNA and RNA that are now believed to profoundly affect what ultimately is produced by the genetic code in the nucleus. They help direct the functions of the cell, the social interactions between cells in tissues and organs, interactions between organ systems—and what a psychopath dreams and schemes and does to others in his everyday predatory wanderings. One way to look at the way the genetic information is actually laid out in the nucleus of cells is quite different from how we all learned it, with all the forty-six chromosomes tightly coiled into their classic X shapes during a brief phase of cell division. Most of the time, that DNA is uncoiled into long strands, like so much pasta in a bowl of Italian wedding soup. The long strands of pasta (the DNA strands) float in a large sea of broth and spices and herbs (transposable elements and other small noncoding bits of DNA and RNA) and the occasional meatball (histones—proteins that act as DNA spools).

These nongene structures are now thought to be at the causal root of some disorders, including schizophrenia, depression, and addiction, as well as many forms of cancer and immune disorders. These elements appear to have been taken up from other organisms such as viruses and bacteria during our evolution, but also from the foods we eat. What was once considered junk DNA prior to 2000 is now known to be far from junk, although many of their functions remain a mystery. The person responsible for this discovery was Barbara McClintock, who did Nobel Prize–winning research at the University of Missouri and Cold Spring Harbor Laboratory on Long Island from the 1920s to the 1950s, although her discovery of the nature of "junk DNA" would not be understood for many decades.

One implication of the existence of these noncoding genetic regulators is that even if we do determine the coding gene combinations that underlie psychopathy, there will still be a million or more combinations of these with the noncoding nuclear elements that we will then need to consider in order to understand the real genetic basis of psychopathy. But we do know some things.

In 2006, I was aware of the warrior gene having a proven effect on aggression and violence, and this allele was certainly on the long list of potential candidate genes associated with psychopathic traits. But this had not been proven, and it was correctly assumed that more genes would impact psychopathic traits. There were several candidates that were known to affect aggression, and these were mostly associated with the monoamine neurotransmitter systems.

The monoamine neurotransmitters, or modulators, as they

are often called, are like volume buttons in the brain. Neurons "talk" to each other by releasing tiny molecules called neurotransmitters into clefts between them called synapses. The signaling neuron releases a packet of transmitters, which can then lock into receptors on the receiving neuron, altering that neuron's behavior. Then the transmitters are broken down or transported back inside the signaling neuron. The two most important neurotransmitters are glutamate and GABA. Glutamate is excitatory, meaning that when it's released and encounters a receptor, it encourages that second neuron to "fire" and send its own neurotransmitters to still more neurons. GABA is the chief inhibitory neurotransmitter, meaning that it tells neurons not to fire. Without it, the brain would go haywire.

Glutamate and GABA form the basis of hardwired behaviors, but if they worked alone you'd have kind of a clunky machine. The monoamines, in particular serotonin, dopamine, and norepinephrine, modulate synaptic signaling and help the machine work more smoothly. These are the transmitters most implicated in psychiatric disorders from schizophrenia to depression and bipolar disorder. For instance, the most popular antidepressants, including Prozac and Zoloft, are SSRIs, or selective serotonin reuptake inhibitors. They prevent the reuptake of serotonin back into the signaling neuron, allowing it to continue doing its job. Less popular types of antidepressant are MAOIs, or monoamine oxidase inhibitors, which block the enzymes MAO-A and MAO-B. These enzymes break down monoamines, so blocking them increases serotonin transmission.

There is a misconception in the popular literature that if one has a "low-serotonin system," one can just ingest more serotonin or take nutraceuticals or foods that will directly increase the amount of serotonin in the brain. However, the brain system is much more subtly tuned with feedback regulation than that. And all the genes that regulate this vast cast of characters interact with each other within a cell's system, and between each other at multiple levels of organization of the cell, the neuronal circuit, and beyond. But in spite of the complexities of the genetics and epigenetics, more and more findings keep reminding us of the power of the genetics, and not the environment, to be the prime mover in behavior.

As mentioned, the warrior gene is a form of the gene that produces MAO-A, and it leads to an underproduction of this enzyme. With less of the enzyme breaking down monoamines, you end up with too much of the monoamines, including serotonin. That sounds like a good thing, but the brain is a complex system and you don't want too much of anything.

It turns out that during fetal brain development, serotonin is released early on, since it is one of the earliest neurotransmitter systems to develop. So if the fetus has inherited the low-activity, high-risk form of the MAOA promoter, less MAO-A will be produced, there will be less of it to break down monoamines such as serotonin, and the fetal brain will be bathed in a higher-than-normal amount of that neurotransmitter. The response of the body, including the brain, to too much of a neurotransmitter or hormone is to try to dampen that chemical's effect. It will produce fewer of the receptors for that neurotransmitter or hormone, and even change the size and cell structure and connections of the brain areas impacted by the flood. Those areas that turn off in fetal development stay pretty much turned off after birth and into adulthood. So this kind of altered brain area will not respond like the average brain when serotonin is released.

There may, in fact, be plenty of serotonin released—let's say after an anger-producing event—but no one is listening. That is, the brain areas that should turn off the anger and rage after a minute or so are permanently altered so that there are fewer neurons to respond, and fewer serotonin receptors to turn on or off. This type of genetic effect that impacts fetal and early postnatal brain development is rather common. No one has definitively shown that the warrior gene causes all this to happen, but it's clear that messing with a neurotransmitter system that regulates emotion should lead to some problems.

Behavioral evidence supports this prediction. It was shown in the 1990s that mice bred to completely lack the gene that produces MAO-A become more aggressive. The Dutch researcher Han Brunner and his colleagues found that several generations of men in one Dutch family had a rare mutation in this gene such that they produced little MAO-A, and these men showed particularly inappropriate behavior and crimes such as arson, exhibitionism, and attempted rape. A wide statistical analysis of boys with the low-producing form of the MAOA gene, conducted by Avshalom Caspi and Terrie Moffitt of King's College London, found that they had greater mental health problems, including ADHD and antisocial behavior, than other boys. Kevin Beaver of Florida State University and collaborators found that males with the warrior gene were more likely than others to join gangs. Compared with their fellow ruffian gang members, they were more violent and twice as likely to use a weapon in a fight. And in a laboratory study by Rose McDermott of Brown University, Dustin Tingley of Princeton, and colleagues, subjects with the warrior gene reacted more aggressively to provocation—while playing an economics game, they were more likely to force an opponent who took their earnings to eat hot sauce.

The warrior gene has also been linked to changes in brain structure. One study by Andreas Meyer-Lindenberg and colleagues at the National Institutes of Health found that in males the gene reduced the volume of the amygdala, anterior cingulate, and orbital cortex—all areas implicated in antisocial behavior and psychopathy—by 8 percent.

The warrior gene's effect is felt mostly by males. That's because it's located on the X chromosome, one of the two so-called sex chromosomes, the other being the Y chromosome. It occurs on about 30 percent of X chromosomes. As anyone who mastered sixth-grade biology knows, females carry the XX sex chromosome combination, while males carry the XY combination. Since a male child inherits only one X chromosome, from his mother, he will definitely suffer if he receives the low-functioning variant, because there is no other gene to counteract it. Females receive one X from their father and one from their mother. After fertilization and early egg cell divisions, one of the X chromosomes in the pairing in a female is inactivated randomly, but for some genes, including MAOA, both remain active. So they need the low-expressing version of the MAOA gene on both X's for them to have not enough MAO-A and thus too much serotonin. Therefore women are not as susceptible to the effects of the warrior gene. Since there is a 30 percent incidence of the warrior gene on each X chromosome, the chances of a female having it on both are 30 percent times 30 percent, or 9 percent. This explains, at least in part, why there are more aggressive males in the population than females. And this difference is increased by the presence of testosterone, which affects aggressive behavior in males more than in females.

In understanding the genetics of psychopathy one might also take a look at the gene responsible for the serotonin transporter, which is a protein that vacuums serotonin out of synapses and back into serotonin neurons for recycling. Near the gene for this transporter is its promoter, the bit of DNA that initiates the transporter's production. A long variant of the promoter that leads to the overproduction of the transporter and thus a decrease of serotonin hanging around in synapses is of considerable importance to the effects of drugs like amphetamine, cocaine, and ecstasy, as well as posttraumatic stress disorder and aggressive behavior in Alzheimer's patients. The high-risk variant of this promoter is also associated with alcoholism, depression, social phobia, hypertension, obsessive-compulsive disorder, and even difficulty experiencing and expressing romantic love. This is not the kind of genetic variant one wants to inherit or pass on.

In addition to serotonin, dopamine appears to play a role in psychopathy. In 2010, Joshua Buckholtz of Vanderbilt University showed that psychopathic traits are associated with greater dopamine release in the brain, and more dopamine means a greater drive to seek rewards. Genes that increase dopamine transmission could explain the addictive behaviors often seen in psychopaths, as they look for more and more stimulation, whether from drugs, sex, or gruesome violence.

Another gene possibly related to psychopathy is the one producing corticotropin-releasing hormone (CRH). This substance activates the body's stress response and often rises just before an addict relapses. CRH in the amygdala is thought to create a profound sense of yearning, loss, and anxiety. This might happen when a loved one dies, when one is under constant anxiety, and when an addict goes into withdrawal, creating another type of "loss of a loved one." For those people who have the low-functioning alleles of genes controlling CRH and other stress hormones, or their receptors, there may be very little effect of stress and anxiety, as is found in some psychopaths.

Normally, amygdala-activated stress will, in turn, end up activating the serotonin-producing neurons in the brain stem. So acute anxiety and stress may quickly lead to release of serotonin, ultimately offsetting the stress. When a normal person is brought to anger, they will soon relax in response to serotonin, which turns off the stress loop. In someone who is an impulsive hothead, the stressor that produces an angry response may not be turned off by serotonin if the brain areas normally responding to serotonin have low function, or if not enough serotonin is released. One's reactions depend on the interaction of all of the serotonin-related chemicals (the transporter, MAO-A, serotonin receptor subtypes, enzymes) with limbic areas. For some, the anger response may go on for hours, not just a couple of minutes. Given all these variables, plus differences in the early development of the limbic structures, all affected by genetics and maternal stress, it is easy to see why there are so many types of stress and anger responses in different people. In psychopaths, subtypes will also exist, but with their underfunctioning amygdala and orbital/ventromedial and cingulate cortices, there is often little stress and anxiety to begin with.

The genes that regulate empathy, and are therefore of great interest in the understanding of the cause of psychopathy, include a range of alleles that affect the function of the hormones oxytocin and vasopressin in the brain. Oxytocin reduces the amygdala's fear response in social situations and allows for trust. It's released in high concentrations during childbirth, nursing, and sex, particularly in women. Vasopressin allows for pair bonding, particularly in men. Voles that have vasopressin receptors in the reward centers of their brains become monogamous. Studies in the laboratories of Elizabeth Hammock and Larry Young at Emory University, Bhismadev Chakrabarti and Simon Baron-Cohen (cousin of comedian Sacha Baron Cohen) at the Universities of Reading and Cambridge, Thomas Insel at the National Institute of Mental Health, Dacher Keltner's and Sarina Rodrigues's group at the University of California, Berkeley, and Paul Zak at the Claremont

Graduate University throughout the period of 2005 to 2010 began to show the role of these alleles in empathy. Paul Zak has recently shown that testosterone receptor genes also affect generosity and empathy.

The empathy and aggression traits and their associated gene alleles have shown some promise for understanding psychopathy, but genes have not been identified that strongly predict other important traits in psychopaths, such as grandiosity, glibness, pathological lying, and lack of morals and ethics. The route to understanding these traits will likely come first through analysis of brain anatomy and alterations in connections in the brain (what features of the brain are involved in these functions?), with the genetic information (which genes affect these features?) coming later.

By 2007 to 2009, researchers began to understand that most complex adaptive behaviors in humans were probably influenced not just by one gene, but by dozens. One lab might find one gene associated with schizophrenia and publish their result. Another lab might find another gene. Other labs would try to replicate these findings but not achieve statistical significance. It was frustrating, and people wondered if a lot of bad data was being published. It wasn't until researchers started pulling together large groups of subjects that they realized there weren't one or two genes responsible but maybe fifteen or twenty, each contributing a few percent of the variance in symptoms.

Most of the genes couldn't be characterized as dominant or recessive, unlike those controlling eye and hair color, for example.

Complex behaviors, which are controlled by numerous interacting genes, are also under the influence of a myriad of regulators of these genes. Aggression, for instance, is a complex behavior, influenced by the interaction of genes regulating serotonin, norepinephrine, dopamine, androgen, and a host of other cellular functions. No single gene can be flipped on or off to decide someone's fate as violent or passive. So *dominant* and *recessive* are not in the everyday lexicon when discussing these behavior-modifying genes and their regulators.

Given the complexity of these genetic systems, any conclusion drawn from determining whether I had the warrior gene (which a thorough genetic analysis would show) would be inconclusive. It would take a whole set of bad genes to faze me.

And I wasn't in a rush to learn about them. Diane's parents had both died of Alzheimer's, so I'd initially been worried about Alzheimer's genes in her and in our kids. But their brains looked healthy and they showed no signs of cognitive decline, so getting our family's genetic results no longer seemed urgent. And learning of my violent family lineage was not enough to supplant the sense of urgency. Two months earlier, I'd been intrigued by my odd brain scan, but the novelty had quickly worn off. Plus I was busy with other projects. Not only had I been giving talks about serial killers, but I was also in the middle of getting two biotech companies off the ground and analyzing brain scans and genetic patterns as part of separate studies of Alzheimer's disease and schizophrenia.

This same time period of 2006 through 2009 was also extraordinarily exciting for our imaging genetics studies. We were hot on the trail of discovering two new genes for schizophrenia and a new one for Alzheimer's, and in developing a whole new method for gene discovery itself. This method shortened, by two orders of magnitude, the time and expense of discovering genetic alleles associated with diseases, especially for the complex diseases and disorders of the mind we encounter in psychiatry. Typically, to locate a gene associated with a disease such as schizophrenia, you'd need something like three thousand subjects. Some of them would have symptoms of schizophrenia and some wouldn't, and a particular gene might be more common among those who do have symptoms. We created a statistical method that uses a set of equations to compare a subject's genetic information with brain-imaging data and psychological testing. This way, you'd need only three hundred, or even thirty, subjects to identify a candidate gene. The technique could also determine which patients would best respond to a drug or other treatment for schizophrenia, Parkinson's disease, or depression, and also quickly determine those patients most likely to have debilitating side effects of these treatments. Instead of a person being a guinea pig receiving different drugs one after another for six months, you'd get to the right one immediately, reducing suffering as well as medical costs.

The imaging genetics lab group of Steven Potkin, Fabio Macciardi, David Keator, Jessica Turner, and several high-end technicians and collaborators across the entire UC Irvine campus was firing on all cylinders at this time, and the drive and need to get papers and grants and patents and talks completed weighed heavily on everyone's minds. Amid this maelstrom of scientific delights, it was all too easy to forget, at least temporarily, about my scan.

And testing for the warrior genes and other aggression-related genes is not a simple process. For instance, there's the GWAS (genome-wide association study), which samples from a few million single nucleotide polymorphisms (SNPs), whose proximate location to genes imply them in the etiology of traits and diseases. This technique is well standardized and relatively inexpensive. But there are significant limitations to GWAS in several important respects; there are more than three billion base pairs total per chromosome (six billion per chromosome pair), so there is less than 1 percent coverage of the genome, even considering SNPs as "proxies" for other DNA variants. Much can be missed with even the best GWAS sampling.

The only way to cover all of a person's genetic code is to do deep, whole genome sequencing of all three billion base pairs, plus sequencing of an alphabet soup of other elements. The cost of such analyses has dropped from hundreds of millions of dollars to several thousand per genome, and there are advertised rates of analysis less than a thousand dollars per person. However, this cost is highly misleading, as that low price comes with no real further analyses, just a listing of the sequences. This is like someone with an understanding of only English being handed a phone book a thousand pages in length written in Mongolian graphemes and Navajo syntax. For several thousand dollars there are commercially available analyses that translate the codes but not the syntax.

This interpretation of the meaning of the codes must still be done by a highly experienced team, including a geneticist, statistician, epidemiologist, cell biologist, and domain clinician (for example, a psychiatrist, cardiologist, or immunologist). This is where the real costs are hidden in full genetic analyses.

The time is ripe for application of sequencing projects integrated with cognitive, metabolic, and brain imaging methods to investigate complex human traits in disorders such as psychopathology in a way that was never possible before. Successful examples exist for complex diseases never previously understood through "omics" medicine, including genomics (genes and related nucleic acids in the nucleus), transcriptomics (various mRNA levels in tissues), proteomics (different levels of proteins and their interactions in relevant tissues), and metabolomics (blood and urine levels of several thousand hormones, metabolites, sugar, etc., and their dynamic interactions over time). Personal genomics and personalized medicine emerge as new feasible applications and not only as future possibilities, thanks to the developments in analyzing genomes and complex traits and visualizing these results into a unified framework.

In any case, it would be a while before someone took the time to give my genes a good looking-over. In the years between sending my blood sample and receiving my genetic results, I did consider now and again what the genetics results might tell me about what my brain scans meant. But I was not concerned about following in the footsteps of Thomas Cornell.

CHAPTER 5

A Third Leg to Stand On

So I had the brain of a psychopath. And I had the family history and possibly the genes of a psychopath. And yet I had turned out very different from the serial killers I'd been studying. Something wasn't lining up, and that makes a scientist look for answers.

Although the loss of specific brain function in my limbic areas was in agreement with the neural profile of psychopaths from my lab and others, I noticed over the following year that there were individual case reports of people with such brain damage who were not murderers or psychopaths. This suggested to me that although the specific type of brain damage or functional loss might be *necessary* to cause psychopathy, it may not be *sufficient* to cause it. Other factors must be present.

Even if my DNA looked dangerous, that wouldn't be enough to turn me to the dark side, either. There was still no real link between genes and psychopathy, only between the MAOA allele and the potential for violence. I looked at all the case studies I could find in the literature and in my work, and saw that for all the psychopaths, including dictators, who had psychiatric reports from their youth, all had been abused and often had lost one or more of their biological parents. While there may be cases where this is not true, I could not find any proven ones. There were cases where the murderer denied early abuse, but many people will deny such abuse, only for it to be discovered later that either they were too embarrassed to admit it, or they were protecting the abusing adult, typically a family member.

It was also becoming known from many studies that there was a high incidence of early childhood physical, emotional, or sexual abuse in the prison population of psychopaths. A small survey of thirty-five psychopathic offenders in youth detention facilities found that 70 percent reported serious mistreatment throughout childhood. Given that the onset of reliable memory for childhood events in adults may reach back to three to four years of age, this implied that a higher percentage of adult criminal psychopaths actually experienced significant abuse earlier than that. As such, it was possible that more than 90 percent of them were abused at some point in their early life. Add to this those psychopaths who protect their abusers, and the percentage could approach 99 percent, or so I reasoned. This was when I first started to consider *why* I might not be a full-blown psychopath. The killers had been abused, and I had not. Despite my hard-line conviction that we are shaped by nature and not nurture, I began to think that upbringing might play a significant role in creating a criminal after all.

The environment can interact with genes during development in a number of ways. One of those is through what's called a genotype-environment correlation. A child with genes predisposing him to aggression may frequently misbehave, drawing hostility and abuse from his caretaker. Or an aggressive parent may pass along genes for hostility and also behave in a belligerent way toward his kids, and then both the genes and the antisocial attitude continue down the line. Such a pattern could explain my murderous lines of ancestors. Even if genes for aggression washed out over the generations, an expectation that families always act like this could have remained.

Another form of gene-environment interaction is what's known as epigenetic marking. Seemingly out of nowhere, your teenage daughter, who doesn't have the svelte shape of you or even your mother, starts to put on weight and looks very much like your grandmother, her great-grandmother. To figure out why, you all decide to take standard DNA tests to determine your respective genetic codes. But it turns out that the DNA code controlling the appetite and obesity of your plumping daughter is more similar to the DNA code of yourself and your lean mother than to that of your fleshy grandmother. So the genetics don't seem to explain your daughter's teenage-onset obesity. And she doesn't eat much more than an average person. Something else unexpected must be going on. Perhaps her metabolism is malfunctioning. But how and why? Then your niece, who is studying genetics in her doctoral work, suggests something may have been passed down from great-grandmother to grandmother to you, and then to your daughter. That something is not the genetic code itself, but a small extra bit, or tag, of chemical information stuck on to several genes controlling obesity and metabolism.

The added tag, called an epigenetic tag, might have been added on to several of her great-grandmother's genes while she was a young child, enduring starvation during a decade-long famine in Ireland, Poland, Bosnia, or the Bronx, nearly a century ago. Her great-grandmother's cellular response to the great stresses of that starvation may have been to change her metabolic machinery to more efficiently use energy and store fat, and to increase appetite once food was plentiful again. So your daughter, her great-granddaughter, under other teenage stressors, and with a plentiful food supply, responded by putting on weight to the point where she now resembles the plump but hearty teenager her great-grandmother became when the famine ended in her homeland eighty years ago. Some of these effects are dependent on whether the ancestor was male or female, since certain genes are "imprinted" on either the paternal or maternal side of the family.

The epigenetic tag is one of many alterations to the genetic code that can be induced by environmental stressors. This is one of the core mechanisms underlying the interaction of nature and nurture.

While there have been numerous recent studies on the role of epigenetic interactions on metabolism, cancer, and susceptibility to infectious and immune diseases, it is also a key to understanding some psychiatric disorders, from schizophrenia to psychopathy. One of my favorite scenes from the 1968 film *Charly* that so affected my career choice is the one in which the cognitively awakened title character goes to his teacher/therapist's chalkboard and writes, "that that is is that that is not is not is that it it is," and asks her what it says. She is unable to decipher the quip, and then he goes to the board and punctuates it into: "That that is, is. That that is not, is not. Is that it? It is."

This puzzle offers a good analogy for what the epigenome does. The raw DNA base pair code in this analogy is "thatthatis-isthatthatisnotisnotisthatititis," and the way this raw sequence is laid out directs the code to be transcribed into the sequence of words but not quite a sentence. Normally the transcribed message from the DNA to the RNA would be translated into the protein, here the mature and sensical sentences "That that is, is. That that is not, is not. Is that it? It is." But environmental stressors can induce epigenetic tags to be added on to some of the original genetic DNA, so that the punctuation, the spacing of the words, the text formatting in general, can be altered to produce a slightly different meaning: "That that is, is. That that is not, is not. Is that it? It is?" Same words, same sequence, but a final question mark added changes the thrust of the message. This slight "epigenetic" change to the sentence's intended "genetic" meaning is different from an actual mutation. In a mutation, the actual spelling of the sentence is changed, either by inserting a letter (or more) or deleting an existing letter. Such a change can, of course, radically alter the function of the sentence, which may now become, "That that is, is. That that is not, is snot. Is that it? It is." In a similar sense, the genome is the book you inherited at birth, the epigenome is the way you read that book.

Another way of looking at the epigenome function is to consider the new car you buy from the dealer. All that original hardware is like your genome, while alterations you might make to soup it up, give it some more pep, or, for your daughter, slow it down, are like the epigenetic modifications.

Epigenetic alterations are one of several reasons why identical twins are not identical. Even with identical raw genetic codes, differences in early environment, whether overly stressful or more positively enriching, can change their behaviors down the line as teenagers and adults. Identical twins can also have different numbers of the same genes inherited from one parent or another, and this can also alter how the identical twins look and behave. A third mechanism can involve a seemingly otherworldly phenomenon caused by "retrotransposons."

Retrotransposons are short bits of DNA or RNA present in the nucleus of the cell surrounding the genes themselves. Once thought to be junk DNA with no apparent purpose, these odd snippets of information are not fixed in place but can move around, like grains of rice in soup. They are capable of connecting widely separate genes, even on different chromosomes, and they can alter cellular function. They can rearrange the "sentences" our DNA types out, and in doing so can ultimately change, usually subtly, human behavior, and account for not only differences in how identical twins act, but also what makes schizophrenics psychotic and perhaps why certain depressives become suicidal.

One of the most common ways the epigenome functions is when environmental stressors, especially early in life, wrap DNA filaments around spools of protein called histones. Stressors can also add or remove minuscule chemical side groups, called methyl and acetyl, to or from genes. These are just small groups of atoms that latch on to DNA strands. Such alterations can stop, slow down, or speed up a gene's ability to be read and do its job. Changing a gene's action alters the amount of proteins that are made, and therefore changes the balance of neurotransmitters in brain circuits, leading to changes in thoughts, emotions, and behaviors. These modifications are a big deal and have become a major focus in the understanding of the interaction of genes and environment, and are the key to understanding the nature-nurture problem. One of the main environmental stimuli that add these methyl and acetyl groups is stress, and these stimuli can include abuse, prenatal maternal anxiety, drugs, and even some foods. Stress releases the hormone cortisol, which transfers methyl and acetyl groups from donor molecules on to DNA.

Such additions may be a key in understanding the etiology, or cause(s), of psychopathy. When these side groups are added or removed from the regulators of the genes, the genes' function is temporarily altered, sometimes for hours or weeks, sometimes for years. Thus, early in-utero stressors like maternal use of alcohol, illegal drugs, or psychoactive medications can alter the later behavior of that child. But stressors occurring close to the time of birth can have the greatest deleterious effects. Furthermore, the later the stressors, like emotional or physical abuse, occur, the less the effect will tend to be. So emotional abuse or abandonment at the age of a year or two is far more deleterious to the child's development and later behavior as a teen and adult than abuse or abandonment at age six or ten.

In perusing the literature on environment and psychopathy, I remembered a classic 2002 paper by Avshalom Caspi then of King's College London and his colleagues, showing what I considered to be the best demonstration of the interaction of nature and nurture. Caspi looked at data from the Dunedin Multidisciplinary Health and Development Study, a long-running study of about a thousand people born over the course of a year (1972–1973) in Dunedin, New Zealand, who have been assessed on several health and psychological measures every few years since they were three. Caspi looked at three factors: whether the subjects had the warrior gene, whether they'd been maltreated as children, and whether they displayed antisocial behavior. (Antisocial behavior was measured by combining a diagnosis of adolescent conduct disorder, convictions for violent crimes, a psychological assessment of a violent personality at age twenty-six, and reports of antisocial behavior from people who knew the subject well.) Caspi found that maltreatment, as expected, increased antisocial behavior. But the increase was much greater in males with the warrior gene. Twelve percent of the guys had this combination of abuse and the warrior gene, but they were responsible for 44 percent of the men's violent convictions, doing four times their share of the damage. Overall, 85 percent of the males with the warrior gene who were severely maltreated became antisocial. A similar pattern was seen in females, though they were less violent. A later meta-analysis Caspi and his colleagues conducted of similar studies showed that even without abuse, the warrior gene does increase aggression, but its effect on its own is much smaller.

Those several months following birth are sometimes called the "fourth trimester," and this extended period of what should have been prenatal development means that early environment for a human infant is particularly important. In fact, the most vulnerable time for a human's brain development in terms of environmental impact is from the period of birth and for several months after, in this fourth trimester. It is in this time that a human needs to avoid serious stressors, and it is when nurturing is so critical. There is a continued need for protection throughout childhood, of course, but the closer to the day of birth, the more important affection is.

Damage to the brain also shapes psychopathology in different ways depending on when it occurs. If at the age of two a child suffers damage to the orbital cortex, which is involved in ethics and morality, he may never develop a sense of right and wrong and may become profoundly psychopathic. If the damage occurs at the age of eight, the person's orbital cortex may have helped other parts of the brain understand right and wrong, but he won't be able to stop himself from committing wrong, as the orbital cortex is also involved in inhibition. If the damage occurs as a teenager or adult, the person will know right from wrong, and other areas of the brain involved in inhibition will be mature enough to help control impulsivity when the orbital cortex fails, but stressful conditions could easily push him over the edge.

Even without specific brain damage, several psychiatric diseases can rear their heads later in life.

The brain's cortices develop in an orderly fashion, with a large chunk of the ventral and orbital cortices developing faster than the dorsal prefrontal cortex during the early and later postnatal period. This means that the limbic, emotional brain starts to mature well before the thinking, cognitive brain. The sex steroid bursts released later, in puberty, tend to "set" the connectivity of these cortices, making them less malleable. Because of this, those preteens and teenagers with delayed development of the prefrontal cortex appear intellectually slower at first. But the flip side of this coin is that development is protracted in many of these late-blooming teens, and their more plastic prefrontal synapses are thought to promote more learning capability over this developmental period. This may be one explanation for the recent finding that apparent IQ can be significantly different in someone who is tested around the time of puberty, and then later in adolescence. Some teens appear to start out with higher IQs and cognitive capabilities, but then regress later relative to their peers in the later teens and twenties. Since IQ is a measure relative to age, this doesn't mean that such people have lost ability, only that as early bloomers they were seemingly smarter than their peers, only to develop much slower than others in the mid- and late teens.

Beyond puberty, the next major prefrontal maturation occurs in the late teens through the early twenties, when inputs to the prefrontal cortex from dopamine and the other major monoamine neurotransmitters, serotonin and norepinephrine, mature. They segregate out into the different layers of these neocortices. When the layering of these neurotransmitters is complete in a person's twenties, the brain is nearly fully mature.

An important corollary to this developmental step is that this is also the time when the diseases involving the monoamines such as schizophrenia and bipolar disorder often display their first obvious symptoms. A typical pattern would be for a college freshman to experience his first psychotic episode during the early winter holiday period. Such alarming problems might be blamed on the rigors and failures of the first big exams, breakups with high school sweethearts, or other such stressful events. But one way to interpret such events is to look at them as inevitable for someone who has the genetic predisposition for schizophrenia, and whose prefrontal cortex is now primed to experience this psychotic break during a major stressful event.

These highly stressful events will likely occur at some point during these years, whether a college term, romantic relationship, or first job challenge precipitates it. Why do stressors precipitate such monoamine-related psychotic breaks? One reason is that stress releases a bomb of cortisol from the adrenal cortex, not only suppressing the immune system, but also blocking the COMT enzyme, especially in the prefrontal cortex. This blocking of the enzyme leads to a surge of dopamine, which floods the cortex and leads to altered firing of the neurons, which in schizophrenia can be associated with poor filtering of inputs, altered signal-to-noise processing by these neurons, and neuronal firing uncoupled from external reality, as well as drastic changes in mood.

There are traits common in different forms of schizophrenia, bipolar disorder, obsessive-compulsive disorder, as well as some of the personality disorders, all developmentally staged psychiatric problems often found in early to late teens and early twenties. Stressful stretches of a young person's life such as college, first marriage, and especially military combat couldn't come at a worse time for the developing prefrontal cortex.

This is a big deal for the armed forces. A freshman and a senior in college are very different human beings. Sending kids to war at eighteen is ridiculous, as they're still in an active state of frontal lobe development. The military uses psychological tests to make sure recruits are not crazy, but that won't tell you how they'll be in two years. If we're going to have war, we shouldn't let soldiers fight until they're twenty-two or twenty-three.

Although psychopathy can also become obvious in the teen years, it can sometimes be noticed in children three and four years old, probably because the ventral system—that is, the orbital cortex and amygdala—develop and mature much sooner in life than the dorsal system. So if there's insufficient activity in these areas—a pattern associated with psychopathy—it will be seen sooner. The principle at work here is that a psychiatric disorder won't become fully expressed until the brain areas involved and their main connections have started to mature. Put another way, you can't break something that is not yet manufactured. Prefrontal development usually ends in the mid-twenties, and the brain is considered to finally come into mature balance of all the circuits sometime in the mid-thirties.

It's hard to codify exactly which behaviors in early childhood indicate psychopathy, but clinicians and many parents say they can see it. What they notice is how a kid will look at you. A child will appear to look right through you, or past you, like he doesn't care that you're there. Such children also show very little fear and can be quite bold. And they'll start manipulating you early on. Some of them, especially girls, can be hypersexual, even as young as five years old, which is often another form of attempted manipulation. In 1963, the psychiatrist John Macdonald proposed three childhood behaviors that predicted violence as an adult: bed-wetting, fire starting, and animal cruelty. The "Macdonald triad" has become well-known, but also much disputed. Bed-wetting is not a great predictor, and fire starting and animal abuse are quite common among boys and can be caused by other factors, such as anxiety or bad peer influences.

Some genes that become risky when a child is exposed to stress may actually be beneficial when the child is raised in a healthy home. Since 2011, three of the journalists and producers of TV shows with whom I've worked contacted me to say that they had spoken to psychologists who had watched some shows I had been on that had included interviews with me and my family. The producers told me that these clinicians said I was, in their parlance, an Indigo child, and also an Orchid child. I had briefly heard these terms in passing and disregarded them as nothing more than New Age pseudoscientific woo-woo. But in going through the list of traits provided to the producers by the researchers, and then comparing them to my knowledge of myself growing up, there are indeed a few similarities. For example, Indigo children appear empathetic, independent, willful, inquisitive, full of purpose, and possessed with a high IQ, with considerable intuition and distaste for authority. Although these qualities register with what I remember about my perceptions about how others saw me about the time of puberty, they could be ascribed to many kids.

Orchid children, on the other hand, are unusually susceptible to early environment stressors and wilt if treated poorly in their youth, but blossom if treated with copious amounts of love. This is, as the description goes, different from the vast majority of children, who are fairly hardy and will do well pretty much no matter what happens to them early on. This particular theory actually may have some biological basis. Kids who inherit the rarer, short form of the serotonin transporter gene, which leads to more serotonin remaining active in synapses, display more resilience to behavioral stressors than those children with the long form of the gene. A similar finding was made in 2009 by Avshalom Caspi's group at Duke University for the gene controlling the receptor for the major stress regulator CRH (corticotropic-releasing hormone).

Testing for these two genetic alleles in such Orchid children would lend credence to the idea that these kids are particularly sensitive to early environment, whether good or bad. And it caught my eye as a gene that I might test in myself. Of even more interest, had my whole family treated me with such a light, positive, loving touch because of something they sensed? People really supported me. I wouldn't have admitted to this a few years ago, but if I were born in other circumstances, I could very well have become the leader of some very bad organization. Come to think of it, I probably would have made a good gang leader.

As a scientist, I'm for genetic testing at birth to determine which kids will be vulnerable to stress, even though as a Libertarian I'm against it. The testing would be a key to preventing more psychopaths. If we have enough markers—genes or galvanic skin response or EEG or something cheap—as part of perinatal care, we'll know which kids we can allow to roam around and get into fights and which need extra protection. Once the tests are done, this private information should be put on lockdown, and then given to parents if they want it.

I don't want to overplay the role of environment in development. Kids learn to do a lot of things on their own without explicit instruction—laughing, walking, speaking. And even more complex adaptive behaviors like personality development happen on their own. Kids are malleable, but mostly at the extremes. In the absence of bad abuse or extreme genetics, kids will turn out okay. There's a billion-dollar business in educational music and games, and some parents put their kids on special diets because they want to control the development of their children, but long-term follow-up studies on these changes in behavior like better performance on spatial tasks, attention span, and hand-eye coordination are rare or nonexistent. People also try to coddle their kids and make sure there's no stress, which is nonsense. Every parent of a grown child knows that no kid turns out how they'd originally thought, and we have very little control over what type of adults our children will grow up to be. Pediatric neurologists I work with have told me this, too. That kid is going to turn out the way he's going to turn out, unless you mess him up royally.

After learning of my brain scan and family history, I considered the role environment plays in development—it was perhaps the main thing keeping me out of the penitentiary—and what that might mean for my theory of psychopathy. There had never been a good synthetic explanation that covered all the symptoms of psychopathy, and part of the problem was that psychopaths have traits that are found in other disorders. Assembling a cogent model would depend on my three decades of knowledge garnered from our lab and other laboratories and clinics, bringing together seemingly disparate cases of brain dysfunction, from schizophrenia to depression to bipolar disorder to addiction to personality disorders.

In the end, my explanation snapped together one Saturday in 2006, while I was nursing a bourbon hangover in my Jacuzzi and doing the *New York Times* crossword puzzle. Struggling for an answer, I tried to relax and just look around. As I scanned our backyard, I saw a three-legged wooden garden stool my mother uses when she comes to the house on weekends to visit, cook, and sit and prune our geraniums. The invigorating effect of pruning the geraniums reminded me of the importance of nurturing, and how too much trauma to the plant would stifle its growth, too little would create a sluggish plant, but just the right amount of stress and care maximized the bloom. This brief moment of observation brought together the elements that created a plausible explanation for the etiology of psychopathy. In my mind's eye that morning, these three elements, and how they interacted, would be represented by that three-legged stool. This formed the basis of my new theory of psychopathy.

The way I envisaged it, the three legs are: (1) unusually low functioning of the orbital prefrontal cortex and anterior temporal lobe, including the amygdala, (2) the high-risk variants of several genes, the most famous being the warrior gene, and (3) early childhood emotional, physical, or sexual abuse.

Since I lacked the early abuse, I continued to believe over the next few years as I gave talks on psychopaths that I was not among them. Colleagues mentioned from time to time that my otherwise well-adjusted behavior (or so I believed) was, at times, unacceptable, but I figured that these colleagues were just mad at something I had done or jealous of some success or attention that had visited me, and they were overreacting.

They weren't.

CHAPTER 6

Going Public

From 2006 to 2008, I stayed focused on my genetics research but gave occasional talks on psychopathy and refined my Three-Legged Stool theory. In 2008, one of my business partners recommended that I attend the Technology, Entertainment, and Design conference, better known as TED, the following February.

I had not been asked up front by the TED producers to attend. I had to invite myself. A week before the TED meeting, the organizers asked the nonspeaker attendees if they had a personal story to tell, since the meeting featured not only the full eighteen-minute invited speeches, but also shorter talks, either two- or three-minute quick vignettes, or seven- or nine-minute medium-length stories. I decided that my Lizzie Borden and brain scan story might be of interest, and so I was asked to give a nine-minute talk. I had a few days to prepare. I had no substantial genetic data to discuss, but I could address at least two legs of the three-legged stool: the brain abnormality and the effects of early abuse. I figured I could infer a bit about my own genes based on the long and multipronged family history of murder.

So in the talk I discussed what I knew generally about the

brains of psychopathic killers at that time. I also discussed the findings from Avshalom Caspi's lab connecting the warrior gene to early abuse. I presented the hypothesis that this behavioral three-legged stool might be the basis of dangerous psychopathic behavior.

I also briefly proposed a mechanism for transgenerational violence, that is, an increase of rates of violence in cultures where three or more generations of children experience societal violence, potentially giving rise to a belligerent warrior culture. The logic would go, I surmised, that in a chronically violent community, girls would prefer to hang out with, and probably mate with, those guys who could best protect them, which would most likely be those boys who carried the most aggression-related genes. And after a few generations the proportion of aggression-related genes may start to concentrate, so that after three or four generations one might start to see a subgroup in a society that is particularly aggressive. This could mean that even if the political, religious, cultural, economic, and social causes of local strife disappeared one day, there would still be a culture of people with a particularly high concentration of aggression-related genes that might persist for centuries. I didn't name names in my talk, but those areas could include Gaza, Darfur, parts of the West Bank, areas of Guatemala and Colombia, and some neighborhoods in American cities.

The last part of the TED presentation explained my Cornell lineage. I decided the night before the event to include my family history because I wanted the talk to be more expansively interesting, and I knew that just going on about the brain and genetics would be too dry and technical for this audience of nonscientists. I was hesitant to open up personal information about my family, but they all agreed it would be fine.

Several months later, the TED presentation was posted one evening on YouTube. The next morning, one of our lab technicians told me there were already 23,285 hits on the video. I had no idea that it was being posted at all, having signed, and forgotten about, the release agreement months earlier while downing my third umbrella drink at the opening party. It had never occurred to me how irresistible the keywords *psychopathic killer* could be. This would not be the last surprise my family would experience in the ensuing weeks and years after that video—and our family's life—went public.

Within a couple of days, in late August, I received two e-mails, and then two calls. These were from head science correspondent Gautam Naik of the *Wall Street Journal*, and Simon Mirren, executive producer and writer of the TV crime series *Criminal Minds* on CBS. They both wanted to pursue aspects of what they had seen in the TED talk. After several conversations by phone and e-mail, it was abundantly clear these two gents were quick studies and at least as bright as my academic colleagues. But unlike academics I knew, these two gentlemen moved fast.

Gautam Naik arranged to fly from New York to Southern California in late October, and hang out for several days with my family and me, at my home, the lab, and an Angels baseball game. He planned to write about my family tree and the genetic basis for aggression.

At the baseball game I pointed to the relief pitcher, Brian Fuentes, and said he didn't have a killer instinct, and probably didn't have the warrior gene. Gautam said that southern India, where he's from, is isolated and rarely attacked, and so the people are docile and might have a low concentration of the warrior gene. He added that India doesn't win Olympic medals because it's a whole country full of Brians.

Gautam was persuasive in convincing me that the family genetic data, however it turned out, would be essential in weaving a compelling yarn about our own twig of the Cornell family tree. So for a month my Italian collaborator and friend Fabio Macciardi did the first of several DNA analyses of the family. My collaborators used a GWAS, or genome-wide association study. For each of us, the test looked at about a hundred thousand bits of DNA related to genes of interest, including twenty or so genes associated with aggression, the MAOA warrior gene among them.

It turned out that nearly all of us had the warrior gene. As for the other genes for aggression, my family members had half of them or fewer. I had close to a full set. It didn't faze me, though, as nothing really does. I laughed it off, like I did my brain scan. I knew I didn't have that third leg of the stool.

Gautam's article and video, which revealed my brain scan and genetic results, ran on the first page of the November 30, 2009, *Wall Street Journal* with the come-hither title "What's on Jim Fallon's Mind? A Family Secret That Has Been Murder to Figure Out: Nature Plays a Prank on a Scientist Looking for Traits of a Killer in His Clan."

Simon Mirren had also contacted me the same day that Gautam had. Within a week he had already worked out a story line for the ninety-ninth episode of *Criminal Minds* ("Outfoxed"). I couldn't believe what he said to me in our second conversation. He had already merged the story line of the serial killer of the episode, basically at high risk to become a psychopathic murderer even as a young child, with the scientific hypothesis I had discussed in my TED talk. He had managed to understand my concept of how the decades and centuries of violence in the Balkans and high-risk genetics would give rise to transgenerational violence and produce a serial killer. And he added the twist that the serial killer turned out to be a woman who beat the odds and had the high-risk MAOA gene variant on both X chromosomes, and had experienced severe violence in her youth. To cap it off, Simon had seen the TED video but once, and wrote that whole story line overnight. After seeing him do this, I never will again say television is infested with knuckleheads. I had met one of the geniuses of TV.

When they filmed the episode, they had me play myself, explaining the orbital cortex and the warrior gene in a lecture hall. The audience included one of the detectives who used neuroscience to help solve the crime. I'm not an actor, but cameras don't bother me. I remember seeing myself in the lens and thinking, "I own you." Meaning I was in control of my performance, and so I owned the camera and the shooting and the audience. That's probably my narcissism. In front of crowds I get amped up, and the energy feeds on itself. It's like a drug to me. One time in 1978, I started lecturing about the kidney and didn't stop for four hours. At the end I got a standing ovation. That happens in conversations, too, and my family has had to teach me to limit myself. When my daughter Tara gets antsy or my wife rolls her eyes, I know it's a wrap.

The combined effect of Simon's *Criminal Minds* episode and Gautam's *Wall Street Journal* article opened the floodgates. From that point and through all of 2010, 2011, and 2012, I would be asked to do more than 120 TV and radio interviews throughout the world. I tried to limit how much I talked about myself and my family because I wanted to focus on the science of psychopathy, but everyone wanted to hear the personal story.

The most embarrassing thing about all this publicity wasn't the fact that the entire world now knew I was descended from a long line of crazy, violent folk, but that I'd become walking, talking proof against my lifelong theory that we are hardwired to be who we are. The idea that I inherited too many of the high-risk gene variants for all sorts of aggressive and weird behaviors, and that my brain also looked like one right out of death row central casting, but that I was not overtly violent should have pleased me, but that was hardly so. I had spent decades preaching about genetic determinism. So my idea that I should have been a very violent person if genes and organic brain state dictate function, combined with the fact that I wasn't, meant I would have to eat a lot of crow in front of my neuroscience colleagues who were fifty-fifty types in the nature-nurture metric. This was not going to be fun. The ribbing and eye-rolling and teasing from my colleagues didn't materialize, to my face at any rate. What happened was worse. Colleagues contacted me, but it was out of concern.

"Jim," my friend Samantha said, "I saw your TED talk video, and did you notice that your orbital cortex and ventral temporal lobe are turned completely *off*?" On a PET scan, lack of activity can look like lack of brain matter, so my neuroscientist colleague Jeffrey said, "Man, you've got a lot of empty space there. Do you have large ventricles?" referring to the brain's fluid-filled pockets. "So many things are turned off. Aren't you alarmed?" And of course I wasn't. Others noted that there was so little activity in the lower, or ventral, half of my frontal and temporal lobes that I appeared to have the brain of someone with a rather severe case of antisocial personality disorder, representing the more criminal traits of a psychopath.

Someone with a brain like this should have very little empathy, and be incapable of bonding with people on an emotional level. Nor should such a brain accommodate sociability, with all the attendant ethics and morality of a normal person.

But one longtime friend from Yale, Dr. Amy Arnsten, who happens to be the leading prefrontal expert in the world, saw my talk and had another hypothesis. She told me that I might possess a gene variant that produces a large amount of a serotonin receptor called the 5-HT2A receptor. (She turned out to be right when I received my GWAS results.) The 5-HT stands for "5-hydroxytryptamine," the simple chemical name for serotonin; the 2 stands for the "2" family of serotonin receptors; and A is a subtype of the 2 family. This type of naming complexity makes some historical and taxonomic sense, since there are now known to be at least thirteen types of 5-HT receptors. To make things worse from both a linguistic and scientific point of view, within each of these thirteen genes that code for serotonin receptors, there are many variants of each gene, which usually means the 5-HT2A gene variant one might inherit may code for a protein that is more or less effective in doing its basic job. The job in this case is to be a receptor protein that grabs on to, or "binds," a serotonin molecule in its vicinity. Amy said I might have inherited a rather potent form of the 5-HT2A gene. And since 5-HT2A receptors turn *off* the orbital prefrontal cortex, a part of the brain responsible for morality and inhibition, the gene variant I may have inherited turned the orbital cortex almost completely off, explaining my brain scan.

So what? Well, my friend knows me pretty well, and she said that part of this genetic and therefore brain function pattern is consistent with someone who is a bon vivant, in other words, a hedonist, a party person, and one who can be charming and appear to be approachable, friendly, even trustworthy, based on what appears to be all-around sociability, even brio and charisma. Such a person exudes confidence. He or she may be someone you may want to pal around with, party with, and have snappy repartee with, maybe even someone you'd want to get closer to. Sounds familiar.

So now the possibilities were expanding at the genetic, brain circuitry, and behavioral levels at a fever pitch. If I had the more rare variant or allele of the 5-HT2A receptor gene, that might help explain my PET scans and behavior. But I knew that the same variant turns *off* the visual cortex, and that didn't show in my

PET scans, and the lack of activity in the front of my temporal lobe didn't really fit with this gene variant. Other things must be going on. There were other serotonin receptors that turn on or off different brain regions, so maybe in addition I had other variants of other serotonin receptors that offset the visual cortex and temporal lobe patterns. (It turned out that I did.)

In 2010, a producer for the Discovery Channel called me—they ring me up occasionally to do shows—and asked me what projects I was doing that year and if they could tag along and film any. I told them I was going to Morocco to the deep desert to interview and collect data from nomadic Berbers and Bedouins as part of our planned "MedGene" project testing for genetics and behavior in previously untested or undertested populations. They were on board and, better yet, put up the money. Fabio and I first attended the World Congress for Social Psychiatry in Marrakech, where we obtained permission to go into the Sahara to test these tribesmen. We also set up collaborations with other genetics/epidemiological psychiatrists from Algeria, Tunisia, Libya, Morocco, Egypt, and Palestine, in part so I could start testing the transgenerational violence idea I had. My son, James (my "lab tech"), and I did the shoot with Discovery over a week in November. After that, James went to a café in Marrakech while I was off in another part of town. A week or so later, a terrorist bomb blew up that café, the Arab Spring went crazy, and our project has been on hold ever since.

But we got the data we needed for the show. Using an interpreter, I interviewed people in each tribe while James collected vials of spit and put them on ice for later genetic testing. These nomadic people couldn't remember any murders, going back at least four generations, so we hypothesized they would have a low incidence of the warrior gene because it wouldn't be very helpful for them in their peaceful communities. Among Caucasians, about 30 percent of X chromosomes have the high-risk MAOA allele. That rate is much higher in Africans and Chinese, and in the Maori. These racial differences have been controversial, and the tribes took a chance with us. What if it turned out that the Arab group—the Bedouins—had a higher concentration? We predicted that rates in both groups would be lower than 30 percent.

We were wrong—rates were about 30 percent, just as high as in Europeans and North Americans. It appeared that the environment might be playing a bigger role than I'd anticipated. In the harsh conditions of the desert, you need to cooperate to survive. If you're violent you could be ostracized, and then you're on your own and you might die. So in this case it was enculturation rather than genetics that was constraining people's aggression. Nurture rather than nature. Another small hit to my belief that DNA explains 80 percent of what we do.

In 2011, I was back on the road discussing psychopathy, violence, abuse, dictatorships, and . . . my own brain, and I started to understand why prior to college I had been so seemingly moral and well behaved and after that had become a different person.

What seems to have happened to my brain at puberty when I developed OCD, and then experienced hyper-religiosity and ec-

centric ideations, was overactivity in the ventral stream circuitry
of my prefrontal cortex. My obsessions with ethics and morality
and my hyper-focused attention are indicative of an overfunction-
ing orbital and ventromedial prefrontal cortex. It is normal for
prepubertal children to be very aware of ethics, morality, and fairness. But as a child enters adolescence the dorsal stream circuitry
of the prefrontal system starts to mature more and more, and thus
the emotionality and hyper-morality of some children gets damp-
ened by the dorsal stream, which processes cold logic, reasoning,
planning, and the practical functions of life. This switching from
the ventral to dorsal stream circuitry should balance one's hot,
emotional, moral-based thinking and feeling to more mature logical reasoning by the end of adolescence. By twenty-five years of
age, give or take several years, this balance of emotion and reason
should finally mature.

I think that in my case, when the normal switching "upward"
toward the dorsal prefrontal stream should have occurred in my
late teens, it did switch up, but then my ventral system turned off,
and my prefrontal cortex stayed in the "up" position for the rest
of my life, greatly favoring my cold cognitive skills at the expense
of my ventral emotional, moral functioning. And it never balanced out like it should have when I was in my twenties. And
while all of those dorsal stream cold cognitive functions thrived,
they appear to have done so at the expense of the ventral circuitry.
So I continued to be social, but I lacked the interpersonal skills
and empathy of most others (a subject we'll return to in the next
chapter).

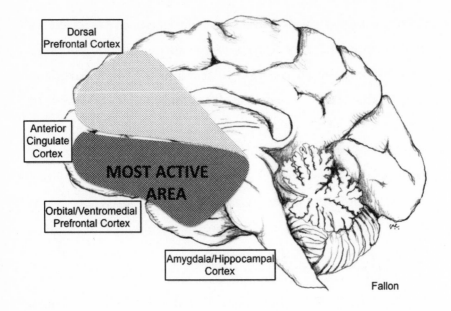

FIGURE 6A: The immature prefrontal system. Normal activity of the prefrontal cortex in a prepubescent child, showing high maturity and activity in the ventral stream circuitry (in dark gray) and low maturity and activity in the dorsal stream circuitry (light gray).

What probably happened in my brain was that around the time of puberty and my early teen years, my ventral prefrontal cortex was more active than normally present at that age, leading to obsessions, hyper-religiosity, and hyper-focused attention, which I did display during that stretch of development. Then, in later adolescence, when the switch should have increased dorsal circuitry and decreased ventral circuitry, leading to a frontal lobe in dynamic balance, something else occurred. The balancing of the dorsal and ventral systems did not occur, perhaps because of a faulty switch in the anterior cingulate cortex. At that point in my late teens, my ventral system may have shut down too much, and the dorsal system may have then overfunctioned. Behaviorally, this may have resulted in my acute executive traits and flattened emotional sensibilities.

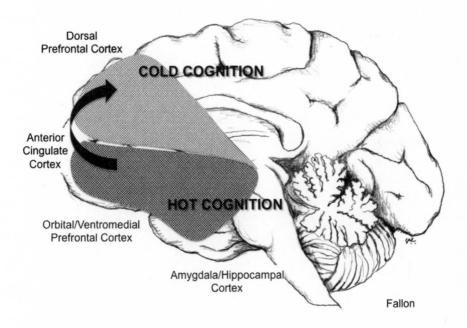

FIGURE 6B: The maturing (and switching) teenage prefrontal system. Normal maturation of the prefrontal cortex system in early and middle adolescence, with maturing dorsal stream circuitry and associated cold cognition.

Note in figure 6E a picture of my adult PET scan showing this unbalanced state in my frontal lobe. This may explain why I have feelings that are muted and lead me to base my relationships more on cold cognition and fairness much more than a normal person would.

So if my dorsal system, responsible for cold cognition and planning, became so dominant halfway through college, why was

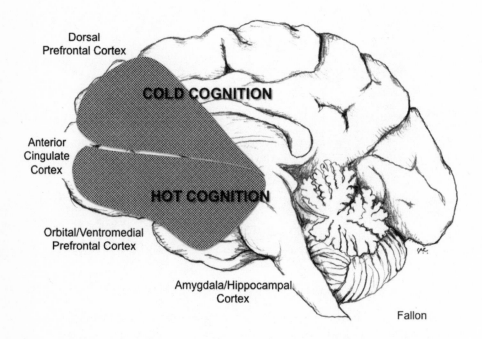

FIGURE 6C: The mature adult prefrontal system in balance. Normal maturation of the prefrontal system in late adolescence and early adulthood, showing a balance of ventral and dorsal circuitry.

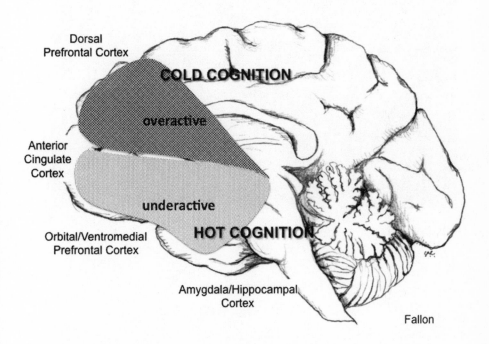

FIGURE 6D: The overcompensated adult prefrontal system. Out of balance after switching from ventral to balanced ventral/dorsal prefrontal system.

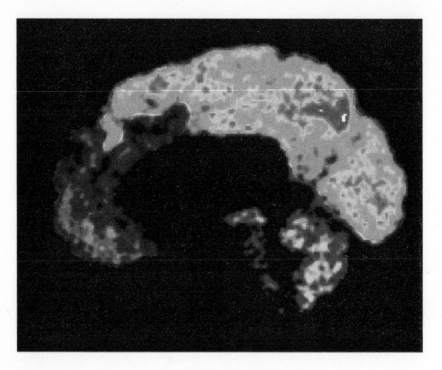

FIGURE 6E: My PET scan.

that the time I became a wild man? Well, I'd always been a class clown and kind of a pleasure seeker. But I'd held myself back, knowing I had an addictive personality. Now, with confidence in my dorsal system's ability to manage my responsibilities, I knew I could party and still get stuff done. And I didn't have my orbital and ventral morality systems to inhibit me.

In early 2013, I came to understand another aspect of my brain. In the Rubik's Cube model, I discussed the different brain circuits thought to form the anatomical basis of behaviors, from attention to memory, language, emotion, and morality. While no one has yet provided the insight to explain how neurons lead to our experience of conscious thought and feelings—the philosophical problem of consciousness—the circuit view of the brain provides some explanations of cognition and can organize data we see in genetics, neuropharmacology, and structural and functional brain scanning.

One recurring feature we can measure in different functional circuits is that for every general function, like perception or emotionality, there appear to be two competing or mutually inhibitory circuits in play. In this book I have focused on the competing interplay between the limbic areas like the amygdala that mediate basic drives such as fear, anxiety, aggression, and pleasure, and the orbital/ventromedial prefrontal cortices that mediate inhibition of these amygdaloid drives, and at the highest level appear to subserve behaviors related to ethics and morality.

In the diagram of the brain shown in figure 6F, the orbital/ventromedial cortex is shown in diagonal hatching, and the amygdaloid cortices are represented as a mosaic of black diamonds. These two areas are directly connected to each other and inhibit each other, as shown by the dashed arrow. Part of the output of both areas is sent "downstream" to the basal ganglia motor areas and serotonin and dopamine cells in the brain stem (not illustrated), but part is sent to the dorsal prefrontal cortex, shown in black. While no one understands exactly how this happens, somehow the dorsal prefrontal cortex, critical for conscious thinking, is able to compare the two outputs and help render a conscious "decision" of how one should act, or not act, in that particular moment. It compares the emotional and animal drives originating in the amygdala circuitry with the social and ethical context originating in the orbital/ventromedial cortical circuit. The connecting strips of limbic cortex aid in this process by adding the important human element of empathy.

Another way to look at this, in psychoanalytical language, is that the ego (dorsal prefrontal cortex) adjudicates the conflict between id drives (amygdala) and the moral context of the superego (orbital/ventromedial cortex). Onto this reductionist view of the brain as a machine, we might say that the dorsal prefrontal cortex

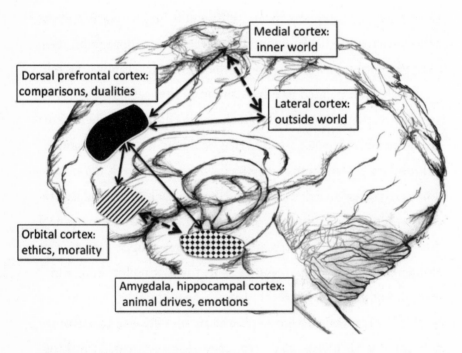

FIGURE 6F: Dualities perceived by the dorsal prefrontal cortex.

"sees" the dualistic nature of the conflict between drives and social context, and makes a decision.

A second dualistic circuit, in our Rubik's Cube brain and the figure just given, involves one part that monitors the outer sensory-motor world that connects us to our external environment. This circuit is located in the lateral strip of neocortex on both the left and right sides of the brain. This circuit is mutually inhibitory with the circuit in the medial, central strip of cortex between the two hemispheres, which is devoted to monitoring emotions in ourselves and others. It overlaps with the "default mode network" that is most active when we are daydreaming and not consciously paying attention to our environment. Like the amygdala and insula, its function is more implicit than explicit. That is, we are often not consciously aware it is functioning. As shown in figure 6F, its two circuits for monitoring the physical world and the emotional world are also mutually inhibitory, and they also connect with the dorsal prefrontal cortex, which helps in deciding which world is most important to pay attention to at the moment. This circuit creates a second duality in our conscious world.

Of particular relevance to our story here is that both the ventral orbital/amygdala circuits in the dualistic circuit on the bottom, and the midline circuit above, are underactive in psychopaths. This is clear in psychopath brains in general, and in my own brain.

How does this manifest itself in the behaviors and attitudes of psychopaths? In late 2012, Anthony Jack of Case Western Reserve University convincingly demonstrated mutual inhibition between the midline (emotional) and lateral (mechanical) circuits. He then hypothesized in 2013 that our brain, by the very nature of the midline versus lateral dualism, limits the way we view reality. These antagonistic circuits view the outer mechanical world and the world of thinking and feeling differently, and this differential "feel" for these two perceptions leads to our dualistic views of mind and body, physical world and mental world. It explains why we see consciousness as something other than just the brain—why we believe in the soul.

Jack's explanation was not only insightful, but it also helped me relook at a mystery in my own life. He provided a new way to look at dualism, and he went on to say that there are people who don't understand the problem of dualism itself.

It has been a bit of a curious thing in my academic life for the past forty years that I've read about and talked with others about dualism. But for the life of me, I could never understand what the problem was to begin with. To me, the brain is like a mechanical machine, like a car, and the mind and feelings are a bit like the speed of the car.

What group of people did Tony Jack find that are stumped by the very idea of dualism? Psychopaths. My lack of emotional empathy and my abandonment of God, the soul, and belief in free will may all be connected.

In 2011, I did another Discovery Channel show, an episode of *Curiosity* titled "How Evil Are You?" For this show, Eli Roth wanted me to scan his brain and test his genes, but didn't tell me why. I knew him only as the actor who played the Bear Jew, the baseball-bat-wielding Nazi-slayer in Quentin Tarantino's *Inglourious Bas-terds.* I told Eli and the crew I didn't want to know any more before doing the analysis.

We took blood and sent it to the lab, and we ran an fMRI scan. During the scan, Roth looked at two types of alternating images, and we collected data on which parts of the brain were most active or inactive. Neutral images were things like dogs or roses, and emotional images included terrorists or people getting shot or beat up. After analyzing the data, I called up my colleague Fabio and said, "This guy is wild. Every time he looks at an emotionally charged scene, all his emotional areas light up. His heart's probably going crazy, and I bet he feels like he wants to throw up." But the midline area, responsible for functions including self-knowledge (discussed earlier), were turned off. So he was very upset but had no idea what was going on. The neutral pictures, on the other hand, lit up pleasure areas, which they don't normally do for people. The genetics showed that he had alleles for high levels of the hormones oxytocin and vasopressin, which encourage bonding and warm fuzzy feelings, and suggested that he'd be strongly empathetic with his family—a great guy to be married to—but his genes also suggested he'd be hostile to people outside his group. I told Fabio, "This guy's a mensch, but you don't want to get him mad at you."

Before giving Eli his results, I asked him, his agent, and his producer, "Are you sure you want this to be filmed?" They said yes, and I let him have it. He went a little white but noted the results made sense. In a conversation that didn't make it to broadcast, he said the first movie he saw was *Alien*, and he threw up in the theater. And when he watches scary movies he has no self-awareness. "Do you know what I do?" he asked. "You're an actor," I answered. He said, "My main thing is I'm a producer, director, and writer of horror films." He's responsible for the gory *Hostel* movies, which are commonly described as torture porn. I said, "You're self-medicating." Making those movies could be a form of exposure therapy, similar to people getting closer and closer to things like spiders, hoping to get over their fears.

Eli added, "I'm awful to work with. I'm tyrannical. People I work with have been telling me, 'You gotta get tested, man, because you're a freaking psychopath.'" But he was a sweetheart otherwise. After the show, we went back to my house. "I don't drink, but I need a beer," he said. "And I gotta call my father and tell him what you just said." He told his father, a retired psychoanalyst, "Dad, I just did the show and Jim told me everything you've always told me." It was hysterical. Based on genes and the fMRI, I could predict what was going on inside his head. It's an antidote to the idea that genetics and imaging are not useful for understanding people. If you just have one of those analytical tools, you can't predict a lot, but together they're very powerful. Knowing about someone's childhood helps, too. Eli's father sent me pictures from Eli's bar mitzvah—the cake was covered in fake blood.

I got a buzz out of that show, predicting Eli's behavior. In some cases you can really nail down what someone's thinking and what's driving him in different circumstances. But this could be dangerous in a courtroom. Going from a useful clinical tool and a nice parlor game to determining someone's life or death, that's a big jump. I've consulted on cases during the penalty phases, but using this stuff when deciding guilt would be jumping the gun. I have nothing against it ethically, but scientifically we're not ready. For instance, Eli's got a wild brain, but he's not a criminal. He's just a talented and different sort of guy. Sounds like someone I know.

CHAPTER 7

Love and Other Abstractions

Diane and I met in late June 1960, the day after school ended for the summer. Although I lived in what was considered the medium-priced end of the upper-class town of Loudonville, Diane lived in an upscale neighborhood of the working-class village of Menands and went to a private all-girls school in Albany. Her father's father, who had grown up poor but had earned himself a good living through real estate, had owned a large swath of Central Avenue in Albany until the crash of 1929, when he lost everything. Thus Diane's father also started with nothing, and slowly created a modest real estate portfolio of his own. He had built the suburban neighborhood in which Diane's family lived, and was a quietly prominent member of the community, having just been elected president of Wolferts Roost Country Club at the border of Albany, Menands, and Loudonville, to which my family also belonged. It was here, at the club's swimming pool, where Diane and I met.

I would go to the pool every day with my younger brothers Pete and Tom, and we would swim and frolic from opening at ten a.m. to closing at six p.m. It was there that the three of us learned to swim, with Pete and Tom excelling through junior high and high school and Tom swimming for the New York State 100-meter championships in his senior year. Like in all sports, I did not excel in swimming but could swim freestyle sprints and breaststroke, just long enough at full-bore to compete for wins, until my asthma would kick in. We also loved to play cards together and with new friends we met at the club, as well as other games we learned from our parents and aunts and uncles, who were uniformly excellent parlor gamesmen.

By July I'd met many kids at the pool, and between games of water polo and "jump-dive" one afternoon, I overheard a girl's voice. She was in the water a few yards from me, but I could hear her say, unnecessarily loudly, "He couldn't be a Fallon. He's too fat to be a Fallon." I glanced over, and there she was, giggling with her friends. When I locked in on her, she turned her head and looked at me with a smile. I was annoyed but intrigued by her self-confident playfulness.

Over the following weeks we started chatting while with our friends, and soon we were sitting at the same poolside tables, often playing cards. We then started swimming a bit together, doing little mini-sprints while playing other water games. In conversation she was clearly ahead of me socially, and while not really being into the shank of puberty yet, and being pretty clueless about sex or romance, I knew I was attracted to her. It was partly her confidence but also her wit and intelligence. We were both just twelve years old, but she seemed to know things, to understand not only her own being, but even a bit of the great beyond, and it really put a hook in me, as I had never met anyone like her. To this day I have never met anyone like her.

At the end of summer, the club threw a dance party by the pool for the teenagers one Friday night. This party was also attended and supervised by the adults. I do not remember the specifics of exactly what happened, but by Thursday my mother and Aunt Flo had encouraged me to ask Diane to the dance, as they must have known that we had taken to each other over the summer. I got to choose my party outfit, an all-white beachcomber knicker ensemble that, fifty years later, my mother and Aunt Flo still have a hearty guffaw over.

The dance party was a blast, Diane and I danced about thirty numbers, and it was all over by eleven. I barely saw, or talked to, Diane until the following June, since she had to go back to school. Her brother Mike and I were good friends, so I would see her when I visited their house, but because I went through puberty late, my fascination with her didn't grow into romantic attraction for some time. Most of our interactions involved me teasing her about the snooty prep school boys she was dating. Summers were magical. Each summer throughout high school we would play at the pool together. We played card and board games and raced each other in the pool, and were captains of our respective girls' and boys' interclub swim teams.

By the end of my junior year, I had finally convinced a girl whom I'd had a crush on for years to go out with me. That lasted about three months during the spring and summer of 1964. Then on August 2 of that year I went over to see Mike, hoping also to see Diane, and she and I ended up going down to their basement family room. We watched TV, talked, teased each other, and then started wrestling like we sometimes did. During one takedown, I got her in a half nelson and then an ankle takedown onto a sofa chair. And for the first time we kissed, and then things started heating up. I'd liked her from the beginning, but at this point I was crazy about her.

We started dating constantly, always hanging out with friends and each other. By the fall of the following year, 1965, I was off to college while she finished her senior year. During that year we really started to talk about things, about what we wanted in our futures. Although we were very different, we shared common interests. But in those discussions it became clear that her entire worldview, and her comfort with that world and herself, was utterly different from mine. In particular, she had no fear of the unknown, no fear of dying or, to my complete astonishment, not existing at all. I could not comprehend her comfort with such a metaphysical perspective, and although she, too, was raised Catholic, she was not particularly observant and had no problem blowing off seeming contradictions in religions and what she felt was silliness in the need people have for eternal life. Her comfort with her whole mortal existence is still, to this day, beyond my reach.

We also learned that we shared a love of children and a desire to have a family early. Our politics were not so very different, although she is more apolitical than I am. Through college we fell more and more in love and tried to spend as much time together as two college students could during New England winters, separated by four hundred miles. She had matriculated at Chestnut Hill College outside of Philadelphia, and I would hitchhike down from Burlington during the winter so we might spend two days and two nights with each other once a month. Although we had been dating steadily for three years, we did not have sex, and that was utter torture for both of us, but a necessary condition of my obsession with being good. Nonetheless, we were in love and had wonderfully romantic and fun times throughout late high school and college, lack of intercourse notwithstanding.

You might be wondering how this story gels with someone who ostensibly lacks empathy or the ability to connect emotionally with others. The truth is, I say "in love," but I've never truly felt fully emotionally connected to Diane. My connection with her emerged partially because I *didn't* connect empathetically. I never understood her. She was fascinating to me, and still is. We have common goals and values—family, Libertarianism, agnosticism— so there's a like-mindedness, but she always felt like someone from outer space. Fortunately, that has always been more than enough for me.

About this time, in the period of 1967 to 1968, my thinking and behavior had started to change. My assertiveness in sports had noticeably increased, and I wasn't pulling punches anymore so as not to hurt people on the football field, and my speed and brinksmanship in alpine ski racing was peaking. I was a bit less kind, and academically I was excelling. It was like an aggression machine had turned on within that year. I had left the Church and my hyper-morality was gone. My classmates were encouraging me to run for class president, and my level of expanding swagger was obvious to others close to me.

In the winter of 1968, my junior year, her sophomore year, I once again hitchhiked to Philadelphia to see Diane for the weekend. I could usually cover the four hundred miles in about seven hours. In the 1960s, there was no problem getting rides, as the Great Fears had yet to grip America. But that weekend the trip through the blizzard took me the better part of a day, including two hours on a farmer's tractor, four hours on big rigs, and many short rides with salesmen and others who had to be out on roads that were otherwise devoid of traffic. More than two feet of snow fell along the way and the wind gusted to more than fifty miles per hour, which made the visibility, let alone the hitchhiking, a bit challenging. I finally arrived after sixteen hours, in the middle of the night. Diane decided to get a motel room near the college. When we met at her dorm, I was completely encrusted in rime. As we kissed, she asked, "Why did you come down here in this blizzard?" Lost for words, I just told her, "I don't know . . . I think it means I love you." A month after my college graduation in June 1969, we were married. We have been together ever since.

Halfway through college, I started to party heavily and my grades suffered. I went from being a six-foot, 220-pound athletic machine to letting it all go, preferring to just have fun. By graduation I had ballooned forty-five pounds. That would be the first large weight gain of my life. My father actually needed to stuff me into a corset to get me into my wedding tuxedo. On the honeymoon I began to lose weight. After the honeymoon, with iffy grades, I had no graduate school plans and no job. I started doing odd construction and trucking jobs, holding a Teamsters' card, then some carpentry, mowing lawns, and bartending at the Saratoga racetrack. I was able to find a teaching job in an all-girls Catholic high school and, as the only male on campus, thoroughly enjoyed teaching those young women. Our first child, Shannon, was born that May 1970, an event that, along with the subsequent births of our second daughter, Tara, in 1971, and then son, James, in 1974, stand out, with marrying Diane, as the most significant events in my life.

I was ecstatic about the birth of our kids. But as soon as they actually came out, I celebrated by going off and partying for several nights. That would be completely psychopathic today, now that dads are more involved. Even then, people looked at me funny, but society allowed it. I didn't feel connected to my kids until they were old enough to start responding as human beings, when they were toddlers. Before that, they were like dolls to me. (Although that might not be unusual for fathers.) Once I got to know them I really enjoyed them, and I do to this day. They were a great source of joy and fascination. Shannon was walking and talking by nine months, and was very entertaining. Tara was quieter and demonstrated early a knack for focus and perceptual awareness of her environment. And it seemed like James was three before he said anything. Then at six or seven he started saying incredible things about the nature of time and God and the universe. Each of my kids is very different from the others.

When they were small, I liked hugging them, playing with them, talking with them. So I was not a distant, cold, aloof father by any means, but my attraction was dominated less by warmth than by entertainment and an intellectual interest. I'm fascinated with other kids, too, but I think a lot are boring. Mine just turned out to be interesting kids, which I'm not saying only because I'm their father—our friends agree.

Following my abrupt change in attitude and aggressiveness in 1968, my connectedness with people, including Diane, decreased. I started to value people for the fun I could have with them, and my feelings for Diane peaked at the end of college. Before that I adored her, but then I started doing and saying things that pissed her off, and I started loving her in different ways. Having children accelerated the shift, as my feelings morphed from passion into admiration and respect for what she was doing as a mother. As I got older I had to learn to re-love people by admiring them. Today I love my kids as friends. I have a lot of respect for them, but I almost forget they're my kids.

Looking back, James says he knew I loved him (I told him so every day). I came to a lot of games and cheered (he won the Orange County sprints, and Shannon and Tara were both Division I swimmers), and he never felt let down by me. I laughed a lot, but I didn't show much emotion otherwise, and he felt a disconnect. I never cried in front of my kids (and Diane didn't, either), and so they tried not to cry or show emotion in front of me. When they saw my brain scan back in 2005, they said it didn't surprise them, and therefore it didn't bother them. One emotion besides joy I did show was anger. It's difficult to get under my skin, and normally if something bothers me I'll shut the door and withdraw, but when I pop it's fierce, and frightening. Nevertheless, James says I've always been his hero.

Another reason I may have been an emotionally distant father was that I was always focused 100 percent on my work. After I graduated from college, I spent a year teaching at the all-girls high school before I was accepted into the master's program in the Psychology Department at Rensselaer Polytechnic Institute, where my academic performance and social life flourished. Those were magical times for all of us, and for my waistline as well. Back in shape in all ways, I was accepted in the doctoral program at the College of Medicine at the University of Illinois at Chicago, where I again thrived in every way, and earned my PhD after three years. A PhD normally takes at least five, but I worked day and night, so my family didn't see me much. I also continued to party. I might work until eleven and then go to a dive bar and enter a dance contest and make some money. I'd come home at five and Diane would say, "I thought you were done at eleven." I'd say, "Well, yeah, then I went out, and look, I won a hundred bucks dancing." It was extreme behavior, but Diane, who stayed at home with the kids, rarely complained about being left alone. I needed only four hours of sleep a night, and I'd use my extra awake hours out having fun. There was no point in coming home to a sleeping family.

Academically, I was armed and dangerous and flying high for my next stint in the postdoctoral program in neurosciences at the University of California, San Diego. These, too, were wonderful years academically and socially, but my drinking and smoking and eating habits continually wore on my athleticism and waistline. Over the period from 1969 to 1978, when I started my professorial run at the University of California, Irvine, my weight, sleep habits, panic attacks, and considerable risk-taking continued to take off some of the glitter of the otherwise good time, often too good a time, I was having.

After more years of the up-and-down cycle in my professional performance and wild weight swings, I decided to chart these oscillations on several taped-together pieces of graph paper. What I saw astonished me. After plotting more than thirty years of my weight and professional and creative output, based on publications, grants, patents, paintings, and other artworks, the correlation seemed too perfect. Whenever my weight peaked, several times going to 290 to 300 pounds, so did my professional and creative output. And when I then had lost all the weight, returning to my peak performance college weight of 190 to 210 pounds, my productivity went to zero, often lasting for a year or two.

The more I ate and smoked and partied, and the less I exercised, the better my performance in all professional fields. And I noticed another thing: When I was on the upswing in weight and then peaking, my ability to communicate on a personal level with people close to me seemed to also increase. While gaining pounds and then reaching my pinnacle, weightwise that is, I seemed more connected to people, particularly family members. Somehow these positive traits, intellectual and creative performance and interpersonal connectedness, appeared always connected one to the other. And when I lost weight, sometimes with the aid of smoking cigarettes, I looked great but was unproductive and lacked any sort of empathy. I became a stud-muffin party boy, perhaps a jerk, on a regular basis. At these times, I especially did not care about how any of my behaviors might hurt other people emotionally or even physically.

I also become more aggressive. Going to baseball games, I sit close to the field and yell at the players (especially A. J. Pierzynski, the catcher for the Rangers), calling them all sorts of names. When other fans complain, I get in their faces: "You wanna fuck with me?" Normally I'm really slow to anger and not physical at all, but when I'm in shape I can tear off the back of the seat. Really, you want to be around me when I'm fat and I've had a couple of drinks. Then I'm a complete sweetheart.

These swings in body and mind, in intellectual and emotional expressiveness, seemed exactly opposite to the way the body and mind are supposed to respond to being in and out of shape. This became a running joke among my friends and me (but not so much to Diane, who was constantly on my case about my health), throughout the 1990s and to this day. I have never figured out why these seventy- to one-hundred-pound swings in weight and behavior occurred, but naturally I suspected abnormally large cycles of activity of serotonin, dopamine, and perhaps the endorphins and testosterone in my limbic system, especially in my temporal lobe and associated limbic/emotional brain where these neurotransmitters, modulators, and hormones were having their greatest convergent impacts. One can guess that alterations in my serotonin-regulated daily rhythms, including those for sleep, were fueling these wild fluctuations, but this is only speculation. Usually my weight swings happen into their own, but sometimes I'll notice that my ass is knocking into the furniture and decide I need to lose some weight, and I do. I've got quite a strong will when I put it to use.

I had only started to wonder in 2011 about how my changes in connectedness fit into these months- or years-long swings in behavior and body type, when I learned, or rather realized, that there might be something seriously wrong with my ability to have normal interpersonal relationships.

Empathy can be thought of in several ways. The first way is to contrast empathy with sympathy. Empathy is usually thought of as being able to put yourself in another's shoes, that is, to imagine that what he is experiencing emotionally is something you have also experienced. Sympathy, on the other hand, does not require that one feels or has actually experienced what one might imagine another is experiencing. Sympathy is more of a recognition that something is eating away at someone, and a desire to do something to lessen her pain. Empathy usually refers to one's emotional reactivity to another individual person. An example of sympathy is when someone hears of the plight of earthquake or flood victims and, although not actually having experienced anything like that, still donates time or financial relief to those victims. This is not to say that the compassionate person responding to this need doesn't also empathize with those victims, only that it is not necessary to do so.

Likewise, there are empathetic individuals who sense that they feel the pain of others but do nothing about it to help the other person. The groundbreaking physiological studies of Marco Iacoboni of UCLA offered a mechanism for how brain processes connect people, at least on an intellectual or cognitive-perceptual level.

The mirror neuron system is a hypothesized cortical brain circuit based on Iacoboni's finding that in primates there are neurons that respond when a person watches the actions of others and when the person performs the actions himself. The superior ability of primates, especially humans, to watch another do something once, and then be able to do the same thing themselves immediately, is thought to be based on the circuit formed between these neurons in the areas of the frontal lobe and parietal cortex.

This system may help to explain why human children can watch their mother do something, let's say fold a towel, and the child can immediately attempt to fold a towel. The sensory motor system that is used to watch the mother do this is the same group of cells that the brain uses to do the task. More difficult motor tasks may also be mimicked effectively by adults using this mirror neuron system.

The first time I lived in Africa was in 1990 to 1991, when I was in Kenya doing research on growth factors in the primate brain under the auspices of a Senior Research Fulbright Fellowship. My brother Tom, arguably the best athlete among my siblings, journeyed from New York to visit me in Kenya. On one of our safaris, he came with me to visit a village in a remote area near the Ugandan border. The shamba man (gardener) Bernard, who took care of my Nairobi yard and gardens, had his family out there, and I had provided him and another family with modern roofing (sheet tin) materials, as the rest of the people in his village lived in small round mud homes covered with thatch. Tom and I had also planned to play golf en route, so I had my clubs along for the ride. Many of the people in his village had never seen an actual white person, let alone golf clubs. Tom and I noticed that Bernard's village had a large three-hundred-yard-long field in the back of the homes, so I had Bernard interpret a question to his neighbors: "Would any of you like to learn how to play golf?" Among the hundred or so of his clan amassed there, a few brave souls stepped forward, including the family elder, a gentleman of about eighty years who was dressed in a full suit and a hat with a red Christian cross emblazoned on it.

They first watched as I flubbed a shot about thirty yards, drawing a chuckle from Bernard and a belly laugh from Tom. Then Tom stepped forward and blasted a three wood to the very end of the field, and there were gasps of awe from the gathered clan. Then the elder stepped forward, grabbed one of the clubs (an implement he had never seen, let alone used before), and took a quick and furious swing at the teed-up golf ball. He whiffed it, but no one made a peep. Then within three seconds, as if clearing a field with a scythe, he swung at the ball again, catching it on the sweet spot, and the ball took off about a hundred and fifty yards, with a hint of a slice. Applause erupted from all of us. Then, one by one, every man, woman, and child stepped forward and each one missed with the first swing, and then nailed the ball with the second. Some of the adult men drove the ball more than two hundred yards.

This was an example of the mirror neuron system cranking away with all cylinders firing. The next year when I visited that village, it was like they had created their own two-hole golf association, an effect I never intended to curse them with in the first place.

This mirror neuron system may help explain why humans can quickly pick up a complex task without any practice. Does a similar circuit, one that interacts with the mirror neuron system, process empathy? Although no one knows the details of such a circuit, there are some imaging studies that point to a consistent set of brain areas that are activated in the laboratory setting that illuminates factors thought to be in play in empathy, and the lack of it. Jean Decety of the University of Chicago, Yan Fan at the University of Ottawa, and Knut Schnell at the University of Heidelberg, among others, have all carried out functional brain imaging studies with fMRI to study the elements of empathy. When we see a happy, sad, or angry expression on someone's face, regions responsible for those emotions light up in our brains, too. Taking the basic mirror neuron system, a cognitive circuit, and adding in areas that are connected to the mirror system but that process emotion, we can envisage a broader circuit underlying empathy. These additional areas include the insula, an area of cortex "insulated" from view by the outer folds of the frontal, temporal, and parietal cortices that all connect to it, plus the emotion-mediating anterior-medial temporal lobe and amygdala, not seen in a surface view of the side of the brain.

Those regions connect with the orbital and inferior frontal

cortices. These three areas are represented in figure 7A that follows. These then connect with and control the hedonism, pleasure, stress, and pain areas deep in the brain, which are bathed in serotonin, dopamine, testosterone, corticotropin-releasing hormone (CRH), and endorphin receptors, as well as vasopressin and oxytocin systems.

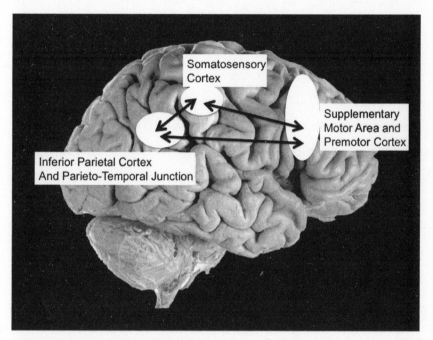

FIGURE 7A: Mirror neuron system.

These hormone and neurotransmitter systems, as it turns out, play a significant role in empathy. Simon Baron-Cohen of the Universities of Reading and Cambridge, Paul Zak of Claremont Graduate University, and Sarina Rodrigues at the University of California, Berkeley, among others, have demonstrated the importance of the genetic alleles that process these empathy-related neurochemicals, which affect a range of empathy-related sensations, from fear, rejection, pain of separation, envy, jealousy, selfishness, and schadenfreude, to the positive end of this spectrum where we find sympathy, pity, compassion, familial and tribal connectivity, generosity, trust, altruism (if there is such a thing), romantic love, and, perhaps, love of country, humanity, and God.

For a comparison of brain activity in the areas that process emotional empathy, refer to figure 7B below. In these three cross sections of the PET scans through my brain, the region of my insula with an abnormal mix of very low and very high activity is identified by the tips of the white arrows. You can't tell in this black-and-white reproduction, but that area is shaded to indicate decreased activity. Another area involved in empathy, the anterior cingulate, also has lower activity in my brain. Meanwhile, the areas of cortex on top of the brain are significantly *higher* in activity in me compared to other people. This may be associated with cold cognition.

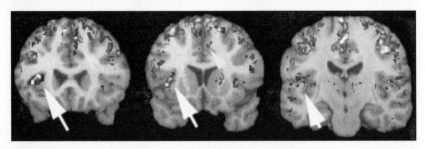

FIGURE 7B: My PET scan.

Given the myriad brain areas and genes involved in what we simply call empathy, perhaps it is not too surprising that the term and its meaning have proliferated into so many different descriptors and their related concepts. We usually associate lack of empathy with psychopathy, and rightly so, because although most psychopaths are not violent, they often treat individuals in a callous, almost numb way—they just don't care. But many express caring for something, and often someone. Even psychopathic murderers will express their love for their parents and siblings, even if those same people were the ones who initially triggered the psychopathic tendencies through abuse and abandonment early on in the psychopath's life. Think of the Buffalo Bill character from *The Silence of the Lambs*, who butchered innocent women without a second thought but became noticeably anxious when his poodle was in danger. But those same psychopaths may hate the rest of society and be out to exact revenge, both violently and nonviolently.

A psychopath whose father lost all the family's money in the stock market or a business deal may exact revenge on the world by directing his antipathy at financial institutions. Terrorists or dictators with psychopathy might seek revenge for perceived slights against their clan, tribe, nation, ethnicity, or religion. But this leaves us with the disquieting notion that the coldest, most violent of our terrorists, lone killers, and dictators have a great sense of "empathy"—an empathy toward their own group, but little toward the life and well-being of others.

Beyond this mix of types of empathy according to individual

versus group (in a sense also related to the dichotomy of empathy versus sympathy discussed at the beginning of this chapter) is another important dichotomy, and that is between emotional empathy and cognitive empathy, also known as "theory of mind." Theory of mind, as I've previously discussed, arises early in childhood, developing progressively until adulthood, and is a key developmental accomplishment in which the child learns she possesses mental states like desires and intentions and beliefs, and that others possess similar states, though those may be different from her own. Someone with autism will not show a normal theory of mind. This lack may also be present in people with some personality disorders such as borderline personality disorder, and also some forms of bipolar disorder. In contrast, people with psychopathy, narcissism, and certain affective types of schizophrenia will have cognitive empathy but lack emotional empathy. These two types of loss of empathy may be associated with underfunctioning of different parts of the lower, or ventral, half of the prefrontal cortex.

Rebecca Saxe of the Massachusetts Institute of Technology has recently shown that theory of mind is centered, in part, in the nondominant hemisphere where the temporal lobe abuts the parietal lobe, the so-called temporo-parietal junction, that is, one node in the mirror neuron system. It is a key spot in a circuit that processes how one perceives the intentions, morals, and ethics of others, a partner to the orbital cortex of the frontal lobe that processes one's own intentions, ethics, and morality. And these two areas of the posterior and anterior cortices connect with each other, perhaps forming the neuroanatomical circuitry for the Golden Rule.

A key question becomes: How does one know if one lacks empathy? If you lack it, there's a good chance you have no idea you lack it, because you don't know what "it" is. This isn't exactly like asking a person blinded since birth what blue looks like, since that person has no reference point at all. But it may be similar to asking a person with color blindness for blue what blue looks like. He can see things that are blue, and blue objects may appear similar to green objects, but blue per se is a mystery. Based on my viewing of interviews with serial killers, it appears that many of them don't seem aware of lack of connectedness. So minus a professional assessment, how can you become aware of your emotional color blindness?

For the first sixty-plus years of my life, I never thought I lacked empathy at all. I was happily married, had a wonderful nuclear and extended family, and a large circle of friends and friendly acquaintances and colleagues—thousands of them—so why would I ever question my sense of empathy? After all, who would want to closely associate and live with someone lacking emotional connectedness?

Before I discovered my brain scan, and even for a few years after, I didn't give a second thought to negative comments about my personality. In 1990, a colleague and I were supposed to give a presentation at a professional meeting, but I blew it off and went to a bar because I knew some cute girls would be there. Miffed, my colleague said, "You're an absolute sociopath to do that." Another time, in Miami, I skipped a presentation to meet up with some gals I'd met and hear a great Cuban band. "You're a psychopath," my collaborator said. "How could you do that?" I told him my car broke down. I knew it wasn't right, but nobody got hurt so I didn't see the big deal.

People often refer to others as "crazy" or "a psychopath" without meaning it literally. Looking back, though, I probably should have paused to consider the sources in my case: trained psychiatrists who specialized in mood and brain disorders and would probably not be so quick to abuse a professional term simply because they were mad.

After reflecting on my brain scan for a year or two, I slowly began to reconsider these statements, and for the first time I thought about what central message my friends and family and colleagues were trying to convey to me.

I realized that I often, in fact, do not directly connect emotionally to people, or understand the way my behavior affects them. I see these things in a cold and distant way, and only upon seeing the effect can I then cognitively appreciate what I am doing. I then realized that my playful teasing of people could actually hurt them, and I was not stopping to read the signs on their faces that they were, indeed, hurt. I was also regularly putting people close to me in harm's way, just for my own edification and for the good times I might experience. It's not like I know exactly what empathy is, but I can now look at behavior—the way people go out of the way for one another, the amount of crying they do—and I can see that I'm really different from most people.

There have been many incidents that provided harbingers of an adult life characterized by a flattening of emotionality and borderline psychopathy. In 1968, I was a witness in a vehicular murder case in Canada during a midwinter jaunt to Quebec City for its storied Winter Carnival. While I was driving from Burlington during a blizzard, my car was passed by two speeding cars, one of which disappeared down the road into the night, while the other went off the road into a ditch, crashing head-on into a tree at about seventy miles per hour. I jumped out of my car and ran down the hill and was just able to crawl through a smashed window to position myself over the face of the driver, who was an elderly gentleman in the throes of death. His chest was crushed and while he was vomiting and regurgitating blood into my face, I kept him revived by mouth-to-mouth for about twenty minutes, until the police arrived. They pulled me out of the man's car by my legs, and I was furious, since I was so intent on reviving him. After testifying at the police station, I ended the interview melodramatically by throwing the old man's bloodied dentures onto the police sergeant's desk. Within a minute I no longer cared at all about the incident, and went on to party heartily in Quebec City, only casually mentioning to my former classmates what had happened. But something did bother me for a long time about that event. I hadn't really cared so much about the dead man after the event, but rather enjoyed the thrill of the whole escapade.

On other occasions I noticed that when people were crying over a tragic or sad event, I had dry eyes and a steady heart rate. I remember when JFK was shot because the people around me were upset; I was more interested in how it went down. One day when I was working at the University of Nairobi, I walked into the morgue and a whole family was standing around a little girl laid out on an iron slab in a white dress. I looked at her and said, "What a nice dress." My attention to the dress rather than the dead girl didn't strike me as odd at the time, but it does now. Even personal injury doesn't bother me. In college I put my arm through a plate-glass window and cut it open from wrist to elbow. I calmly looked at the tendons with an anatomist's eye. These incidents should have told me something wasn't exactly right about all of my emotional responses, or lack of them. But how could I have known that my brain wasn't normal?

As I've continued to examine my own behavior and personality, I realize that my relative lack of empathy complements my overall competitiveness—since I have little emotional regard for the feelings of others, I have few qualms about doing whatever it takes to win a competition or persuade someone to do what I want. Even when they were young, I never let my children win at anything, and now that they are grown, they have started mercilessly beating me at games, especially Scrabble. As you might surmise, I am a sore loser. Playing Scrabble, I might mislead people and lie about what I'm planning, to set them up. I don't think I cheat—it's no fun to cheat. It's much more fun to manipulate (a prime trait of psychopaths). I'll win fair and square but still stick it to them. I taught my kids that games are best played in a ruthless way—it's all about the aesthetics of winning. And I argued that ruthlessness respects your opponent, but that's bullshit. I also just have to win. It's narcissism, ego, pure competitiveness. To some degree that competitiveness runs in our family, thanks to the warrior gene(s).

Fortunately for those around me, my intentions are rarely malicious. In other words, I don't get my jollies from doing harm to other people; I simply don't feel that bad if I happen to hurt someone while in pursuit of my own goals or even amusement. I love a good practical joke, and even though I don't do anything dangerous or illegal (usually), I know when I've unintentionally hurt someone's feelings or embarrassed them. But I haven't much cared. I've also been known to lie in order to gain the confidence or trust of the person I'm talking to. It's part of my persona of gamesmanship, a way of coping with life so that it is never dull for me. But the lie is most often the leaving out of information, rather than adding untrue information. For example, if someone asks me what I do, I might say I've been a bartender and truck driver but am now semiretired. Although technically true, the overall point is a lie, one I might use depending on my read of a person and what I want from them, which may only be to impress them with my high intelligence for a truck driver.

This is true of some psychopaths, but they're all different. Some come from bad families and lash out angrily because their fathers beat them. Most are numb, and it takes a lot to stimulate them. Like an addict, they have to do more and more to get a buzz, they need more and more extreme experiences to feel anything. That can be expressed positively, through romance, or, if they've been abused, revenge. There can also be a developmental miswiring in the brain concerning sex and violence due to sexual abuse, which can lead to rape. The area is not well studied.

More often than not, my manipulation of people has to do with my own pursuit of adventure and pleasure. I'm always in search of a thrill or good time, and I've been known to put other people in compromising positions all for the sake of a little rush.

In 1990, I finally took a sabbatical from my laboratory at UC Irvine. Biomedical research scientists typically do not take them. Sabbaticals break up the flow of research and the training of students in the lab, so they end up being extremely counterproductive. But our children were getting to the ages when they would soon be leaving for college and getting married, and we would lose the opportunity to take a grand trip together. I wanted to go to a place exactly opposite of Irvine, California, so we spun a globe and East Africa came up. I applied for a Senior Research Fulbright Fellowship, received it, and we were off to Nairobi and the Serengeti. I scored some brain research equipment to set up labs in the School of Medicine at the University of Nairobi for nine months. The family went there together with me for six weeks, then returned to California. While there, I was privy to several disconcerting conversations concerning the suspected origins of the deadly hemorrhagic Ebola and Marburg viruses, and HIV/AIDS.

In that first year of my sabbatical, two physicians at the Nairobi Hospital told me about a man who, in 1989, had been brought in from a remote mountain site, bleeding out from most of his bodily orifices. Within a week he was dead. It was quickly determined he had visited the Kitum Caves in Mount Elgon in the west of Kenya near the Ugandan border. I recognized the name of the caves: for thousands of years matriarch elephants led the herd deep inside them under the cover of darkness to scrape away at the walls to get at the salts and other minerals they need to thrive. This is a place I had always wanted to visit, but the story put a bit of caution into me. The man had contracted Marburg hemorrhagic fever, caused by the Marburg virus, a close cousin of the Ebola virus with similarly deadly results.

When my brother visited me that December, we went on a safari to the west and northern sectors of Kenya. I decided to finally visit the Kitum Caves. I wanted the sense of danger, but told Tom only about the elephants. When we arrived at the Mount Elgon National Park entrance gate, the place looked deserted. Tom ran into the ranger's hut, and the park ranger told him that with some troubles on the mountain and the increasing activity of armed Ugandan rebels in the park, no visitors had come to the park for nearly a year. To me this meant that we would see an unprecedented number and variety of game, as the entire mountain was devoid of humans. So on we went, unafraid of any danger, man-made or not.

We reached the only place where we could make camp. I did not want to tell my brother that this was the same small campsite clearing the ill-fated man had stayed at just a few weeks before he died. We collected an enormous pile of firewood and started a fire in the clearing at dusk.

Night arrives at the equator like an ax dropping. Within ten minutes of sunset, the hyenas started in with their banshee yelps.

Within an hour we heard, or rather felt, the thumping of elephants foraging two hundred or so yards away. By about eleven that night, we could hear two lions growling and several more spine-chilling taunts from a hyena. We decided we needed to take some action to shoo away the larger critters, so we both grabbed large flaming branches from the fire and started to wave them around while we yelled plaintive cries. This was a scene out of the film *Quest for Fire*, and remarkably it worked. The woods around us fell silent and we wrapped ourselves in blankets and curled up around the fire.

After an hour the forest came alive again, with what seemed like every lion, hyena, and leopard doubling and redoubling their efforts to get us, and our fire, out of their clearing. The closer the animals approached, the closer Tom and I wrapped ourselves around the fire, which was gradually losing its fuel. As the older and larger brother, I had managed to gain an inside position closest to the fire and kept inching around so my back, neck, and head were always inside his body. I tried to reason with Tom that since I had a wife and kids, perhaps it was more prudent to allow the first lion or leopard or, worse yet, hyena that showed up a shot at him before me. This close-quarters strategic and tactical positioning of our respective bodies went on all night. By the next morning, we were alive but absolutely spent.

We arose quickly, made coffee on the remnants of the fire, and checked the clearing to see that three of the big five game animals had indeed visited us that night, but without incident. We drove to the path leading up to the Kitum Caves and noticed that many of the saplings along the trail had been freshly stomped down by the herd of elephants that had passed us at some distance during the night. When we arrived at the cave entrance, an intense odor of feral urine and feces nearly knocked us over. We saw thousands of trail and spoor signs of at least a dozen mammals at the cave entrance. As we walked in, a fine spray of multiple grass-filtered waterfalls bathed us, much as they showered the elephants on those magical, noisy nights. Deeper into the cave we could see where elephant tusks had gouged out fresh crevices for salt and mineral mining by the herd. In some areas huge slabs of the cave wall had fallen, blocking our passage in spots. As we entered the last sunlit area of the cave, the skeleton of an elephant that had taken a misstep in the dim cave light lay twisted in a deep crevice. And there, we heard them. As they approached, the din became a deafening cacophony of screeching and the manic flapping of ten thousand wings. In seconds they were all around us, thousands of Egyptian fruit bats we had disturbed. We decided to make haste out of there, getting as far from the caves as we could, and head north to Lake Turkana to look for human fossils at Koobi Fora.

Two years later, back in the safer arms and approved odors of Orange County, I received a rather animated call from Tom. Apparently someone had given him a copy of Richard Preston's *New Yorker* article "Crises in the Hot Zone" and the 1994 book *The Hot Zone* (later adapted into the film *Outbreak* starring Dustin Hoffman), and he was furious. He had correctly guessed that I purposely had taken him on the exact trail from the campsite to the caves where the man had contracted Marburg and died. Suffice it to say, he was livid at me for putting him in harm's way. "It was a great experience," he told me, "but I can't forgive you for bringing me to that place."

This was not the first or last time I would put the lives of people close to me in danger. Whether this is a sociopathic behavioral pattern is of some interest in late-night family discussions around the living room fireplace. To some this is just an indication of an adventurous person sharing his favorite jaunts. But to the people who have been enticed by me into going somewhere without being privy to all the serious dangers involved, this behavior goes way beyond an adventurer's sense of play.

I think the best way to characterize my specific lack of connectivity to people is that I live in an empathetic flatland. While I do have a modicum of empathy, I tend to treat everyone the same, whether they are family members or complete strangers. Like in that bar fight I pulled my buddy out of. I thought it was unfair for the other guy to whale on my friend as he ran away, and also unfair to hold the other guy down so my friend would whale on him. Friends think I'm disloyal because I don't stick by them through thick and thin, but I think I'm just fair. If they're wrong I'll tell them. Meanwhile, my family always wants me to reach out to them more, initiating contact, or at least pay more attention to them than other people when we go out. People close to you naturally desire to be treated in a very special way emotionally, and not being able to deliver that connectivity from the heart can be a big problem for such relationships.

My friendships are less pure than most. A lot of people would say I'm very giving, and that I do a lot of helpful things for people, but a chunk of that motivation is so I can call on them later to do a favor for me. I can call up busy, well-known people I've helped out and say, "Would you like to do something for me?" and they do it in a second because I've built these connections over the years. People would say that's just good business practice, but the problem is I do this with people without really caring about them. I'm like a Mafia don. When I saw *The Godfather* way back when, it seemed eerily familiar. If you ask people, they say I do good works. It doesn't end up being pernicious; no one ends up feeling used or slighted. It's just not an honest friendship.

The way not to manipulate people is to ask for something in return almost immediately. Guys will do things for women and want sex right away. And you don't manipulate people by snarling. You do it by being sweet as shit. I'm able to use my personality and some amount of charm, techniques that come naturally to me. Early on I saw my friends, brothers, and other male family members get in trouble all the time by fighting, and they never ended up getting what they wanted. To me they were dolts, inelegant, boorish. It's more fun to manipulate people without violence.

Many people, if I told them, "I'm doing this for you so I can use you," would still probably find that okay, because they know I wouldn't do something mean to them. Friends have said, "I know you're using me right now, but I don't care." They think I'm fun and I hang around interesting people, so they'll put up with it. Some people close to me who know my motivations don't like it. They want a real relationship. My wife wants a real marriage.

In 2002, Diane was diagnosed with non-Hodgkin's lymphoma. She was pretty sure she would die, and at times during chemotherapy she wanted to. I was diligent in providing her a nutraceutical green tea, which remedied the side effects of chemo. She considered my assistance a big deal. It showed I cared. However, in 2008 I carelessly engaged in a series of flirtations that went nowhere but ended up deeply hurting Diane. She made her feelings known, but since nothing actually happened between me and the other people, I did my usual thing and blew off their significance. I understand better now how much pain my indiscretions caused her, so I will not elaborate on them further. Understanding my power to hurt other people does not come naturally.

In many ways, I can appear empathetic. I'm a good listener and I like to hear what people are about. But I often do this because I'm trying to find a way into them. Bars and racetracks are great equalizers—I'll go and chat with people and not mention that I'm a professor. I'll be very open and tuned in to them but always will be thinking in the back of my mind, "How can I play with them? How can I get this girl to say, 'I want to have sex with you right now,' or how can I get this guy to say, 'Do you have any businesses I can invest in?' or how do I get this person to say, 'I trust you with this private information'?" Gaining that kind of access requires empathy, but it's just cognitive empathy, theory of mind.

I don't always use the information I'm given; I just get a buzz when people completely open up to me and make themselves vulnerable, especially when they've only known me for a few minutes.

Often, I'll actually try to help them. If they have a problem, I'll say, "Oh, I'll hook you up with this doctor or that investor." But the raw motivation is to have them in my hands. People become little experiments to me. I get fun out of talking to people, but to say I really care about them would be going too far.

When people drink, they're more likely to open up, and I think that's why I like to drink so much. When I'm drinking I feel connected, and that feels good, but mostly because I like having domination over people. I don't act on it, because I don't have to. If I didn't have enough going on in my life already I might be a bad guy. The potential is there, but I have so many other things—family, friends, research, businesses, media appearances—that I don't need to go any further. Maybe some guys will need to pick up a woman and take her home, but if some chick just says, "Do you wanna do it now?" that's enough for me. The sex has nothing to do with it. I'm a terrible flirt, and Diane knows this because she knows how women respond to me. Women of all ages will surround me, and I'll listen to them. I know the games. Their boyfriends and their husbands don't listen to them, so I do. I don't use those situations to the advantages you'd associate with psychopathy, though. I don't take it down the darkest dark road.

That's what makes me what I call a "prosocial" psychopath. Our patron saint might be Bill "I feel your pain" Clinton. Of course, I can't diagnose Clinton as a psychopath, but he appears to have several key traits and is probably at least a 15 on the Hare Checklist. Having sexual relations with a college-aged woman who works for you is universally scorned but common, and denying multiple affairs is hardly psychopathic on its face. But there are his many microbehaviors that we've all seen him do in various forms many times. As the blogger John Craig points out, when Clinton saluted the troops it was with a mock flair, when he was applauded he gushed mock humility, when at a funeral he seemed to appear appropriately somber, and then felt the need to display tremendous grief, always bravely holding back tears. Gentle sobbing might accompany his hearing of the newest poverty statistic. The nonpsychopathic person makes up stories, but only someone with real psychopathic traits will pull these stunts time and time again, with such high stakes, and never step out of character. The former kingmaker adviser to Clinton, Dick Morris, said that his former confidant was devoid of empathy, adding, "Hillary loves Bill, and Bill loves Bill. It gives them something in common." A hefty swath of the country, particularly in his own party, still loves him. And despite a political rift that separates us, I like him, too. He is my kinda guy.

One of my favorite pastimes is to guess the individualized brain circuitry and genetics of different people I know, or even people I've just met. Going backward from their personalities and various cognitive and emotional traits and subtle tells, I try to guess how their unique neural machinery operates. I'm also asked to do this in reverse for colleagues and legal teams. After testing the genetics and brain imaging data of a person I otherwise know nothing about, I'm asked to explain what their traits might be, and whether they have a psychiatric disorder such as Alzheimer's disease, schizophrenia, depression, or psychopathy. I'm pretty good at figuring out such things and offering a diagnosis or description of the person's traits. I get the same sort of buzz out of doing this, and of finding out that I'm correct, as I do when I'm trying to handicap winners at the racetrack. These are the games I like best.

In 2010, I was asked to predict what, if any, unique neural circuitry and genetics would characterize the garden-variety Libertarian. This question was posed to me during a show for ReasonTV. *Reason* magazine is the flagship publication reflecting Libertarian ideas and ideals, and after hearing that I was a Libertarian, they slipped that question into an interview on psychopaths, free will, public policy, and individual liberty. After the usual caveats ("No one has ever studied libertarians in this way, so I don't know"), I played the thought experiment I so like to engage.

My guess is that the Libertarian brain is one in which the upper or dorsal cortical areas are more highly functioning than in the non-Libertarian person. This would be associated with the higher than normal rational and cold cognitive approach to problems characteristic of Libertarians. The Libertarian brain might also have lower than average insular cortical activity commensurate with the somewhat reduced level of interpersonal empathy seen in many Libertarians. That is, Libertarians rely more on a sense of fairness and justice than on how they feel emotionally about a person or a group of people. Jonathan Haidt of New York University has studied Libertarians and reported with colleagues in 2012 that they indeed are more rational, less emotional, and less empathetic than Democrats and Republicans.

Libertarians, like agnostics and atheists, tend to have a low crime rate, so the neural machinery most associated with a sense of ethics, the orbital and ventromedial prefrontal cortex, would be expected to be normal to above average, while their animal drive system involving the amygdala and limbic cortex might be lower than for the non-Libertarian. These circuit factors would be associated with a person with high self-control and low animal drives.

In personal reflection, this pattern fits with my own behaviors in my late teens and early twenties, when I first chose Libertarianism and agnosticism/atheism as political and religious mind-sets. As a Libertarian I would prefer many situations where some people die. I don't feel responsible for individuals dying as part of a broader cause and don't think we should spend every dime we have to save one child. Such coddling will end up destroying the human race. And who adjudicates who gets coddled? I look at the distant horizon, how things will play out in a hundred, a thousand, ten thousand years. If one person croaks tomorrow for the sake of society, it's too bad, but I don't care. I wouldn't let a kid starve right in front of me—I'm not a monster—but if I ran the government I would cut out all welfare.

I haven't heard a lot of Libertarians admit to these views, but if pressed I'm sure many would agree. For me, by sticking to the basic principles of the Constitution—fairness, private property, and so on—I know some people will die, but it doesn't bother me.

If the system weeds out weak or lazy individuals, fine. I don't want to encourage unproductive or irresponsible behavior because I think it will kill society. I'm more sympathetic to the species than I am to that one person or group of people.

There are others who have cared more about larger causes than the people next to them. Many great humanitarians were, on a personal level, apparently not so nice to be around, and seemed to have little interpersonal empathy while simultaneously displaying a great depth of empathy for the poor and downtrodden. Mohandas Gandhi, one of my few heroes, may have been a pill to be around, and even his wife, Kasturba Gandhi, talked about his cruelty to her and their children. (See *The Forgotten Woman* by Arun and Sunanda Gandhi.) Another heroic figure of the twentieth century, the consensus saint Mother Teresa, was reported to be cold to the people close to her, including the children she helped. Donal MacIntyre, writing in *New Statesman* in 2005 ("The Squalid Truth Behind the Legacy of Mother Teresa"), and Christopher Hitchens, discussing in his 1995 book *The Missionary Position*, both point to the seemingly substandard and even cruel treatment of the children she saved. While these claims are controversial, they do illuminate a type of global empathy toward humanity. An empathy that saves thousands, but perhaps is impersonal to the point of disregard and even cruelty to the individual humans being otherwise saved by a great humanitarian.

Oddly, seeing a neurologically impaired child in pain really gets to me. I played myself as a mad scientist in the Russian movie *Dau*, about the Nobel Prize–winning physicist Lev Landau, and during the filming I started to tear up when they rolled in a cage full of crying babies. When I saw two who had neurological disorders (fetal alcohol syndrome, Down syndrome), I almost unraveled. This reaction to children with developmental disorders goes back to my youth. A sister of a friend of mine had Down syndrome and that stuck with me. When I was delivering drugs for my father's and uncle's pharmacy, I would run into more children with developmental disorders and they seemed to be distressed. So I think this is one case where I had strong empathy early in life, and it stayed in my emotional response repertoire while other emotions faded. It may have become a conditioned response triggering sadness, because I don't have that for any other people.

My involvement with charity and good works is predominantly with complete strangers, or just acquaintances of people I know. Diane and I give a lot personally and anonymously to charity. I think it's our duty. And I do a lot of work for charities as an adviser and a lot of service work on committees, and I refuse to take money for it. To me it's part of my role as a state-paid professor. I will do this at the same time I am leaving my best friends and family members in the lurch. I have excuses for this behavior, but even I don't buy them.

The fact that I give to charity may seem to go against my disagreement with welfare. But welfare allocates resources from people who have earned them toward a long-term system that does nothing to encourage its dependents to leave it, so in the long term it's a complete failure. Meanwhile, I'm not so callous as to ignore the fact that there are many destitute people starving on the street, and certain well-managed charities are great at helping them get on their feet. In Africa, I saw need, so I spent money on housing and medical and educational supplies. But I had to do it secretively so I didn't attract opportunistic parasites.

I have become more aware of my lack of empathy in recent years, but sometimes my subconscious does the work for me. These moments come out of nowhere, most often and most vividly in dreams. The dream this one particular night in 2008 woke me up and left me in a daze because the feeling associated with it was so intense, and because it seemed to arise from a part of my brain that was silent when I was awake.

Here is the four a.m. note I wrote to myself about the dream:

I was on a journey and found myself in the Irish countryside. I came upon a large garden party at a comely mansion and decided to enter through the back gates and as I roamed through the party I came into a cavernous main party room, a sort of dark wood-lined beer hall. Someone asked me what I was looking for and I said, half jokingly, "the truth." . . . I offered that my sense of love and truth and beauty had been a somewhat opaque mishmash until my wife had developed lymphoma. I then became infused into the imagery from where I spoke. As I continued, Diane and I went through this transformation, and we became embedded in this illuminated plasma, on our backs. This very comfortable and sweetly illuminated plasma was actually the layers of a watercolor and pastel painting within which I was embedded. And as I lay on my back, within the painting itself, the colors of the painting started to dissolve and washed around me in pure and mixed spectral hues, spinning and washing off, layer by layer, in this most beautiful kaleidoscope of swirling, wonderful colors. And then the last layers of colors finally washed off this huge painting I was part of and I was left, lying on my back on the plain white canvas. And I asked myself, "Where is all the truth and beauty and love?" and what this was all about. And I turned my head to the right, and there was my wife Diane, lying next to me. And in and through this moment of epiphany, I saw true love and was completely happy. The guru and his friends at the table all raised their hands and yelled, "He found the answer," and then the trinity of wizards all floated off.

The dream happened in the middle of a year or two of particularly bad behavior on my part, and it probably got to me. At that moment, I knew exactly how I felt about Diane and how my lack of empathy can inadvertently damage such a gift as her.

And yet the dream didn't stop me. The devastating series of flirtations mentioned earlier happened soon after.

CHAPTER 8

A Party in My Brain

In 2010, the Norwegian Consulate invited me to give a talk on depression at a small two-day meeting. I had spoken about the subject several times before and had taken special interest in how psychiatric disorders—including depression, bipolar disorder, and schizophrenia—can affect creativity. Here I planned to talk about the usefulness of combining imaging and genetics and psychological testing into mathematical models to understand psychiatric diseases like depression, and I would build up my case by first talking about personality disorders. I figured this would be an excellent venue to test out my Three-Legged Stool hypothesis about psychopathic murderers and psychopaths in general in front of some world-class psychiatrists known for being both learned and circumspect—a potentially tough crowd. I was confident about the hypothesis scientifically and also happy the theory got me off the hook, since I didn't really believe I was a psychopath.

The Oslo symposium was titled "Mental Illness: Bipolar Disorder and Depression." The symposium was interesting for several reasons. In Norway, as in much of Scandinavia, people are hesitant to admit to, or discuss, the fact that they or others in their circle of family and friends have a mental disorder, particularly depression. Ellen Sue Ewald, director of education and research at the Norwegian Honorary Consulate General in Minneapolis, and Reidun Torp, a noted Alzheimer's disease expert at the University of Oslo, took on this national problem by organizing this meeting, and invited one of the top clinical experts on depression in the world, Hossein Fatemi of the University of Minnesota, to discuss the medical and psychiatric issues surrounding the different types of major depression and bipolar disorder. Ewald also managed to convince former prime minister Kjell Magne Bondevik to talk about his own struggles with bipolar disorder, which first afflicted him during his first term. In 1998, Bondevik had demonstrated considerable bravery and leadership in publicly admitting his condition, and had taken a leave of absence to start therapy. Against the odds, he'd then gone on to serve a second term and enjoy an overall successful tenure. This had been a breakthrough.

The night before our talks, Dr. Fatemi and I met to try to coordinate our lectures. Fueled by the hypomanic energy I always get before a talk, plus a couple of vodkas, I ripped through my PowerPoint slides. As I sped through them on the computer, I glanced up at Hossein, who had a curious look on his face. He had recognized the hypomania, my pressure of speech while I was talking to him, and based on this amped-up kineticism he suspected something I had never even considered before. Hossein explained that I might have bipolar disorder. That conference would be the first time I seriously considered the chance that I may actually have a mood disorder. I had heard ten years prior from a close friend and colleague of mine, a noted neurologist, that he had only learned of his own bipolar disorder from a fellow neurologist; he had failed to see his own disorder, a common occurrence among neurological and psychiatric clinicians, especially in their early years of practicing medicine.

The revelation that I may have had bipolar disorder most of my life without realizing it floored me. A long-term clinical colleague and friend, Adrian, a psychiatrist and neurophysiologist, had remarked in 2005 that I had an unusual EEG pattern that showed a unique alpha rhythm. An alpha rhythm is a synchronized firing of neurons in the range of 8 to 12 Hz, or cycles per second. Mine was a very high-voltage, single-frequency rhythm that reached into my frontal lobe, as shown in figure 8A. At the top are two color maps of the alpha wave "coherence," with much of a normal person's alpha coherence being present in the occipital lobe, at the back of the head. My alpha coherence, on the other hand, is intense in level and spread over much of my occipital, temporal, and frontal lobes. The actual alpha rhythms of a normal person versus my own are shown in the lower part of the figure. A normal alpha peak tends to be somewhat wide, spread over a frequency range of 9 to 10 Hz, whereas mine is very high in voltage with a narrow spread confined to about 9.7 Hz.

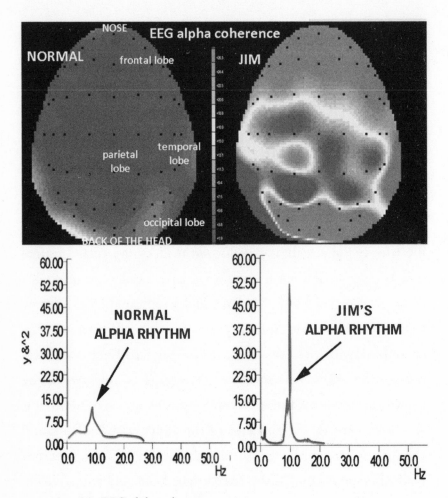

FIGURE 8A: My EEG alpha coherence.

He'd said that this pattern was consistent with a sort of highly focused, meditative Zen state, but also was indicative of a significant risk for depression, although he didn't have an explanation for that association. Of course, I reveled in the whole Zen brain aspect and blew off the depression part, a typical reaction of denial. Many clinicians who have known me well for decades have always remarked that I am clearly hypomanic. This is a wonder-fully elated state of being, in which one feels like one is being continually pumped with sunshine all the time. I would get into this state for many days or even weeks at a stretch. It is the type of disease no one ever wants to be cured of. It feels wonderful, and those of us with it feel great all the time, though we're prob-ably quite obnoxious to those around us. The idea that this exu-berance could be associated with bipolar disorder was theoretically acceptable to me. I already knew that bipolar disorder is defined more by the bouts of mania or hypomania than by the episodes of depression.

Thinking about this kept me up all night, and it ultimately changed the way I view disease. I also reflected on various episodes in my life, looking for signs that I might have missed before. I had never considered myself depressed, though I have experienced nu-merous episodes of dread, generally associated with some metaphys-ical and existential crises. They started when I was about nine and are characterized by an overwhelming rush of negative thoughts, followed by utter dread. They last fifteen to thirty minutes, during which I cycle through a series of thoughts about mortality, God, the afterlife, the concept of the soul, and the meaning of existence, and eventually arrive at the conclusion that nothing at all matters and life is not worth living.

They're not fun, but at least these episodes last only a few minutes. (Two of my kids and one of my grandkids also get them; we call them the "death yips.") Until that day in Oslo, I never considered that these were anything more than my emotional response to my obsession with death and mortality. It never occurred to me that they might be a symptom of depression.

Most of us assume depression is the result of external tragedies, or of stress or dark thoughts, but often episodes of depression happen spontaneously in the brain and then lead to those dark thoughts. Similar phenomena happen to us all the time. For example, it is likely that nocturnal emissions cause the sleeping ideations we call wet dreams, and not the other way around. Another example is how we think of free will. While we all think that we first plan our actions and that they are then willfully carried out, in some cases a part of our frontal lobe may actually "decide" first, unconsciously, that we will perform an act, and after we carry out the act we fool ourselves into thinking we planned it. In other words, we are fooling ourselves into thinking we are in control of our actions. This is how the need for a comforting, or at least logical, narrative can occasionally drive our conscious existence. Our body and brain work in harmony to decide what to do, and seconds later we may tell ourselves a story that we actually meant to do it.

The day after discussing my slide presentation with Dr. Fatemi, I gave my talk at the University of Oslo to a mix of politicians, media, students, neuroscientists, and psychiatrists. After considering the serotonin and inferior temporal and frontal lobe imbalances in my brain the night before my Oslo talk, I had added some additional slides. In one, I showed an illustration of the brain, identifying an area that can lower mood by reducing dopamine transmission in other areas. This region, called the subgenual cingulate gyrus, may be chronically "switched on" in people with depression. The neurologist Helen Mayberg of Emory University found that you could immediately treat major depression by turning it off using deep brain stimulation (DBS), a technique that involved threading an electrode deep into the brain. Reduced activity in this area is associated with psychopathy, which may explain why you don't see a lot of major depressives who are also psychopaths.

After some anatomical slides, I presented a slide listing many of my clinical, subclinical, physical, and behavioral phenotypes (my actual traits and disorders). I also listed my risk for related illnesses through an ingenuity "network analysis" that takes into consideration all of my genetic alleles, the interaction of these genes, and what diseases and traits are inferred from this network. I had just received these results, as a more thorough follow-up to the genetic results I'd received two years prior for the *Wall Street Journal* article. It confirmed that I had many of the genes for aggression, but added more detail on genes related to several other conditions.

On the left of the slide were all of the syndromes I've had in my life, and their age of onset and age of offset where appropriate: asthma, allergies, panic attacks, OCD, hyper-religiosity, hypertension, obesity, essential tremor, addictions, hypomania, high-risk behaviors, putting others at risk, impulsivity, insomnia, flat empathy, aggression, hedonism, individualism, creative bursts, and verbosity. Next to that list of traits and clinical conditions, were statistical estimates of how at risk my genes put me for particular disorders, including various neurological, psychological, behavioral, endocrine, respiratory, and metabolic disorders. The phenotype-genotype pairings matched up very well. (After examining the nightmare combination of genes I inherited, Fabio had said, "It's surprising that you ever made it through fetal development, let alone your adolescence." I could have been another of my mother's miscarriages, or a case of teenage suicide.) At the end of the question-and-answer period of the talk, in which I never mentioned my own potential depressive episodes, the chairman of psychiatry said that, based on my genetic information and my energetic performance, I appeared to have a subtype of bipolar disorder, thus confirming Hossein's suspicions from the night before.

In the six years of personal discovery I had experienced since my brain scan, this was the first time I was really stunned. I realized I had never had a clue about the deeper groundwaters that had shaped me. Later that evening at a post-symposium, at the home of my dear friend of thirty-five years the polymath neuroscientist Ole Petter Ottersen, *rektor* (president) of the University of Oslo, I talked with other clinicians, and they supported the idea that I had been bipolar all along. One called my rather revealing personal lecture a "Lutheran confession." For the life of me, I still do not know what that means. But afterward I started to think that my firm denial of God was a product of, rather than a cause of, depression. (Now I'm not so sure about God; maybe there is a God and an afterlife after all, who knows?)

Thanks to great feedback from circumspect neuroscientists

and clinicians, the Oslo trip had firmed up my confidence in my Three-Legged Stool theory. But somehow I had "contracted" bipolar disorder during the trip. Like Wile E. Coyote running off a cliff, I hadn't seen the reality of my own bipolar disorder until I slowed down long enough to recognize the gravity of the situation.

I learned much about the clinical intricacies of depression and bipolar disorder listening to Dr. Fatemi and his lecture during those two days in Oslo, comparing the clinical picture with the neuroanatomical circuits I had drawn up for the talk, and further fleshing out my knowledge of the disorder after I returned home from Norway.

The National Institutes of Health's *A.D.A.M. Medical Encyclopedia* defines bipolar disorder as follows: "Bipolar disorder is a condition in which people go back and forth between periods of a very good or irritable mood and depression. The 'mood swings' between mania and depression can be very quick . . . In most people with bipolar disorder, there is no clear cause for the manic or depressive episodes. The manic phase may last from days to months." Since the age of nineteen, I have displayed 85 percent of the listed symptoms during my hypomania, including little need for sleep, reckless behavior, elevated mood, and hyperactivity. In the depressed phase people usually experience sadness, difficulty concentrating, fatigue, low self-esteem, and hopelessness.

Depression is a complex mix of mood disorders that, taken together, affect 10 to 15 percent of the global population at some point in their lives, making it one of the most common psychiatric maladies. Becoming depressed as a result of a loss of a spouse, child, friend, or career is, of course, normal. But depression may occur in the absence of any clear environmental stimulus, and in many cases runs in families, suggesting it is, at least in part, genetic. The key feature differentiating bipolar disorder, formerly called manic-depression, from major depressive disorder (MDD), also known as major or clinical depression, is the presence of hypomania or mania that cycles with the down or depressed moods. There are other types of depression such as seasonal affective disorder (SAD), typically found in people with a brain rhythm dysfunction that acts up during the dark winter months; postpartum depression (PPD); dysthymia (a mild, long-lasting form of depression); and melancholic depression, in which the person is unable to experience pleasure, a condition referred to as anhedonia. There are some severe forms of major depression, including catatonia, in which the person hardly ever moves, and psychotic major depression (PMD), in which the person experiences not only depression but also hallucinations and delusions.

My personal concern, however, focused on the bipolar disorder that was mentioned in passing over the years by close friends of mine who are also clinical psychiatrists and neurologists. I always discounted such suggestions for the simple fact that I never considered myself capable of the normal depressed feelings the average person experiences, other than perhaps the sense of dread I experienced at times starting in my youth, and the wildly disorienting and bizarre emotions accompanying the regular panic attacks I experienced starting when I was eighteen. Instead, my adult life had been replete with a riot of positive feelings, pleasurable mayhem, ecstatic bouts of whimsy and creativity, and a rollicking good time on almost a daily basis. The extent and intensity of my positive moods throughout adulthood after graduating from college were either a buzz to those around me, or annoying to others since I always seemed to be having a good time. And I was and still am.

This assumption that my almost chronic, overly positive mood was not indicative of bipolar disorder was, perhaps, a form of denial on my part. I saw depression as a form of weakness and didn't want to admit that I may be a victim. Meanwhile, who in their right mind would ever want to cure hypomania? It feels great, even if one does appear to be, as an eloquent neurologist friend put it, a "fart on a skillet"—volatile and unpredictable.

Bipolar disorder is now considered a spectrum disorder, which means in part that we don't yet fully understand what it is. The two principal types are bipolar I, which features extended periods of mania, and bipolar II, which is characterized by hypomania, a less intense version of mania. There are also minor forms III, IV, V, and VI. Bipolar I is more serious and debilitating, since the highly aroused, aggressive, and agitated state of mania can include psychotic delusions and hallucinations, paranoia, and behaviors highly damaging to one's relationships, job, and bank account.

My biologist colleague Rob and I once compared his clinical mania with my hypomania. I told him that my days- to weeks-long bouts of hypomania were associated with little sleep, bursts of productive creativity, and a desire to party hard. He contrasted this with his manic episodes. He said a typical one would last a week and involve him walking out of his lab and jetting to Vegas, where he, too, would spend all day and night gambling and partying, but he would also buy thirty TV sets, jewelry, and expensive household items he didn't need. Such a week would set him back more than fifty thousand dollars. This behavior also led to divorces and a severe disruption of his career numerous times. He also said that although the manic phase felt wonderful, his creative output was large but not of high quality, something that contrasted with my hypomanic experiences.

During some of my episodes, I would end a late drunken Jacuzzi party at my house and drive off to Vegas with one of my three like-minded buddies, and spend the weekend there drinking and gambling like there was no tomorrow. Diane found my disappearing acts incredibly inconsiderate, and worried about drinking and driving and other dangerous behaviors. (The kids never complained; they just thought their dad was different and did crazy things.) In the end these shenanigans also threatened my friends' marriages, and I eventually lost my comrades. Basically, their wives told them they couldn't play with me anymore. One wife of a colleague, a Nobel laureate, pulled me aside at a party and pleaded with me to not hang out with her husband anymore. Another wife told me I reminded her of the scene in *The Great Gatsby* in which Nick narrates his final feelings about the Buchanans: "They were careless people, Tom and Daisy—they smashed up things and creatures and then retreated back into their . . . vast carelessness . . . and let other people clean up the mess they had made." It was never clear to me whether my friend's wife was referring to my hypomania, or to something a bit more sinister. After some tricky times, all my playmates have gotten over the marital rifts I played a part in causing.

Psychiatric conditions often carry with them a phenomenon called comorbidity. This refers to the presence of other disorders in addition to the primary one in question. So a patient diagnosed, for example, with bipolar disorder or schizophrenia will often have other diagnoses, too, such as borderline personality disorder. I don't know anyone who is just a psychopath and nothing else. There's wide overlap between disorders, in the symptoms displayed, the brain areas responsible, and the transmitters involved. And my psychopathic traits can't be discussed in isolation because other problems shape how they're expressed. I'm attractive to people in part because I'm bouncy and glib and I can bullshit my way around. Well, that energy and fluidity comes from my hypomania. So all my behaviors are tied together.

Doron Sagman and Mauricio Tohen of the Lilly Research Laboratories in Indianapolis have written that people with bipolar disorder are at higher risk for panic disorder, OCD, and substance abuse. In addition, about one-third of bipolar disorder patients, but not major depressive disorder patients, also exhibit antisocial, borderline, histrionic, or narcissistic personality disorders. These people are also more likely to commit suicide, be obese, develop type II diabetes, and smoke.

This list of bipolar comorbid ailments recently gave me pause. This was a familiar "who's who" of friends throughout my life, starting in my childhood and continuing, alternately, through my teen and young adult years. I had the full load of the symptoms associated with these disorders, and each one of them dominated some phase of my life, with one peaking, say, in my early teens, only to be replaced by another full set of symptoms. In each case, I had displayed long bouts, up to years, of at least 80 percent of the symptoms for each disorder. Another curious thing was obvious in the clinical symptom reports and comments told to me by senior family members and clinicians. Most of these disorders were strongly impacted by the serotonin system, and to a lesser degree to the other monoamines, including the dopamine, norepinephrine, and histamine neurotransmitters. But serotonin and the temporal lobes jumped off the pages. My life, however hypomanic and wonderful, was a serotonin catastrophe, and one that screamed of a lower temporal lobe in distress. And if the lower, or inferior, temporal lobe (including the amygdala) was in distress, then the inferior frontal lobe and its connection in the insula would be a bit out of whack, too. This wackiness was evident in my PET scans—as Amy Arnsten had suggested after seeing my TED talk. My psychological world was starting to make sense.

After Oslo I continued to think about other ways my funky monoamine system explained my experiences. In a panel event titled "Madness Redefined" at the 2012 World Science Festival, the depression expert and author Kay Redfield Jamison, the psychiatric and legal expert Elyn Saks, and I talked about why so many people with bipolar disorder display such bursts of creativity, and how they are overrepresented in the arts, music, theater, and sciences.

During the hypomanic stage, monoamine transmission increases, and these neurotransmitters put you in a positive mood, so you want to create something, and they can also boost connectivity between different areas of the cortex, allowing for novel associations. The creative impulse is one reason mental illness can sometimes be viewed as a blessing, especially in cases of mild bipolar disorder like mine, in which one benefits from the joys of hypomania without the devastation of full-on mania or depression.

The temporal lobe, and the orchestrations of its perceptual and emotional memory function, is also heavily influenced by monoamine neurotransmitter systems such as norepinephrine, dopamine, and, especially, serotonin, which all modulate the circuits to enhance and diminish sensory inputs. My own genetics show an unusual mix of high-risk alleles that code for enzymes and proteins involved in the monoamine pathways. But high risk for one type of malfunction can also confer low risk for another function. For example, one allele that codes for the growth factor BDNF (brain-derived neurotrophic factor) is associated with excellent memory but high anxiety. This is the combination I have, and it fits with my actual behavior. The other allele of BDNF codes for lower memory function but also low anxiety. So what would I rather have, a great memory and high anxiety or a poorer memory and a mellow disposition? Tough call.

The lower temporal lobe, beyond its role in emotional memory, fear, anger, rage, and anxiety, also has a role in insight, a sense of the supernatural and God, and the feeling that one is experiencing extrasensory perception (ESP). These purported "psi" abilities include precognition, clairvoyance, presentiment, psychokinesis, and similar such silliness. Patients with temporal lobe epilepsy report ESP experiences before epileptic episodes. The sense of the supernatural and the reporting of experiences beyond this spatio-temporal plane are common in these patients, in schizophrenics, and in hallucinogenic drug users. These supposed psi experiences are treated by clinicians and researchers as subjective symptoms of a disorder, as opposed to objective signs of real capabilities.

Belief in such far-out experiences such as ESP is called "magical thinking" in psychiatry and is considered a symptom of some underlying disorder such as schizophrenia, irrational fears, or obsessive-compulsive disorder. Beyond the serious psychiatric stigma associated with magical thinking are common taboos and superstitions and generally accepted practices such as prayer. One person's magical thinking may be another's deeply held religious belief system. But when a psychotic person, perhaps one experiencing a psychotic break associated with bipolar disorder, MDD, or schizophrenia, starts hearing voices that tell him to murder someone, the temporal lobe issues can transform from personal belief to extremely serious public menace. Delusion-driven murder is not typically seen in primary psychopaths, who carry out their predatory behavior without such hallucinations or emotional involvement. There may be some psychopathic killers who do experience violence-inducing hallucinations, but this type of motivation and behavior would most likely be due to a psychopath having a comorbid psychotic, rather than psychopathic, condition.

I have clear memories of a perception, perhaps one that could be classified as temporal-lobe-based, serotonin-induced, and almost spiritual. The perception started when I was about three years old, although they may have begun even earlier. Each night as I lay on my back while starting to doze off with my eyes closed, I would sense, and then see, a vast black-silver sheet forming in the periphery of my vision. This sheet would start to fill inward toward the center of my visual field, and then contract to a bright point as it rushed toward me. The point of light would accelerate toward the center of my forehead just above the brow line, and when that point of light energy struck me, it simultaneously felt as if it were of infinite mass and infinitesimal size. That point would hit me with a "ping," as light as a feather, but containing what seemed to be the entire mass of the universe. The experience was weird and wild and I always thoroughly enjoyed the near-mystical sensation it imparted.

Once in the late 1960s, while driving back to college in the middle of the night with a friend of mine, I saw some strange silver-green light pulses reflecting off the windshield molding of my VW bug. It was so strange that I pulled over to the edge of a cow pasture and got out of the car, strolling into the black winter night. My friend and I looked up and witnessed the most intense display of the aurora borealis, or northern lights, seen in that area in decades. I felt like an ant standing on the stage of a vast theater, looking up at a stage curtain that would shimmer intensely, then shoot and disappear into a single point, seemingly to the deepest reaches of the universe. This was much like the nightly childhood experience.

Later that year in my college physics class, I first learned of John Wheeler's description of a black hole, and I realized that what I was sensing as a toddler was like falling into a black hole. That was a satisfying and tangible explanation for that wonderful feeling created by the chemicals in my head.

CHAPTER 9

Can You Change a Psychopath?

The experience in Oslo motivated me to try to put this whole psychopath business to bed once and for all. The Oslo psychiatrists and geneticists had convinced me that I had a type of bipolar disorder characterized primarily by hypomania rather than depression, and the full genetic workup I'd had done before the meeting provided overwhelming evidence that something was wrong with my empathy hormones and monoamine systems. It was time to take a closer look at my personality.

Personality and character are different. We all have a common sense of both, with "personality" being the repertoire of traits such as emotionality (e.g., neuroticism, anxiety, avoidance), extraversion, agreeableness, openness to new ideas and experiences, and conscientiousness (carefulness, diligence, self-discipline, and a drive for achievement). "Character," on the other hand, is less obvious than personality. A person's true character can only be determined when he is placed in a quandary, a stressful situation that forces him to make a hard decision.

Scientists tend to think of personality as more genetically driven and immutable, with the character more malleable to stressors, experience, choice, and belief. The character arc of heroes in novels and film is one such example of deep character change for the better. Our beliefs in religion, government, family, and civilization are, in part, based on this hope that an errant person's character can be saved from the "dark forces of evil."

Humans are inherently interested in figuring out who they are. Just look at the size of the self-help section of your local bookstore. In trying, as individuals, to come to grips with our own personality and character, we might try to assess our own emotions, actions, and desires through introspection. Though, since we are biased—in some cases favorably, in others less so (as the saying goes, we are our own worst critics)—we might not get such a reliable picture, and suddenly we're off trying to become president when, in reality, we have terrible judgment and no sense for diplomacy. Consider one study of the million students who took the SAT in 1976: 60 percent said they were a better-than-average athlete (a statistical impossibility), 70 percent said their leadership abilities were above average, and 85 percent said they were better than most of their peers at getting along with others. A quarter of them thought they were in the top 1 percent of getting-along ability. So it would be no surprise if I saw myself as more likable than I really was.

When I returned to Irvine, I started to ask everyone I knew—friends, family, colleagues—exactly what they thought of me and of how I treat people. I told them to hold nothing back, to tell me the truth, and to pull no punches. About half of the people responded. The others chose to say nothing or just laughed.

In the opinion of my friends, was my behavior really all that bad? Two of my closest friends are Susannah, my first postdoc research partner at UC Irvine, and Mark, her husband. They've known me intimately since 1977, and Diane and I still have dinner at their house. Mark told me, "Jim, I love you, I really do, and I have a great time with you, but I can't trust you. I know I could never count on you if things get really bad." I asked him if he could be specific. As was the case for most of the other fifteen friends who gave me answers, he was disappointingly vague. He said that if given a choice between staying with him in a tight situation and having a good time doing something else, I'd go for the good time. He knew this because he had seen me do it over the years. He would invite me to a party at his house and I would always give him the runaround, refusing to commit to his party until the afternoon of the event to see if another, more exciting opportunity would crop up.

I approached a number of psychiatrists, psychologists, and neurologists who have known me well for years, some going back several decades, and posited the same queries. As I mentioned earlier, several of my colleagues had questioned my behavior on various occasions, sometimes calling me a psychopath. But I'd brushed them off, preferring to attribute their comments to jealousy or anger rather than consider that these behavioral specialists may have a point. I had worked closely with these people, broken bread with them, traveled with them, and I felt I was close with all of them. Every one of them told me the same thing. They said they had been telling me for years what they thought of me: that

I was a nice and interesting fellow and great fun to work with, but that I was a "sociopath." I told them I was sure they'd been kidding. They said they had been dead serious with me all along.

What everyone seemed to be telling me was that I was Psychopath Lite, or a prosocial psychopath, someone who has many of the traits of psychopathy other than the violent criminality, a type of psychopathy in which one finds socially acceptable outlets for one's aggression and which is manifested in a cold, narcissistic manipulation of people. On the Hare Checklist, I have three of the four factors—the superficiality, the coldness, and the unreliability—but not the antisocial tendencies.

I continued to ask my close friends what they thought of me. The bottom line was that I seem to be a nice guy, usually, but that I occasionally do things to suggest I don't really care about other people. Consider the words and phrases they used to describe me: "manipulative," "charming but devious," "an intellectual bully," "untrustworthy when it comes down to you or me," "narcissistic," "superficial," "unreliable when you're needed," "egocentric," "unable to love deeply," "shameless," "completely lacking scruples," "cunning liar," "no respect for laws or authority or rules of society," "live by a selective moral code," "irresponsible," "completely unfeeling," "cold," "unempathetic," "emotionally shallow," "The Great I Am," "pathological liar," "blame others," "completely overblown sense of self-importance," "constantly bored," "looking for a buzz," "a need for constant stimulation," "fearless," "irresponsibly puts others at great risk with yourself," "very popular but with many shallow relationships," "no sense of guilt whatsoever." Good grief, Mrs. O'Leary, other than that, how's your cow?

In hindsight, I shouldn't have been surprised. Throughout my career I have often been asked to participate in psychological tests, generally to help colleagues gather research for their own studies. Between my twenties and forties, I took three formal psychological tests, the results of which align with one another. The most comprehensive one was conducted in 1994 by my colleague Stanley, a professor finishing his second doctoral degree in clinical psychology. The test report is nearly fifty pages in length and is actually made up of a number of different tests that examined my intelligence, personality, and mental health. I took them over a three-day period at my home, through interviews, paper forms, and various tasks measuring reaction time and short-term memory.

Much of the report is in psychometric jargon, but some of the summaries give a pretty clear picture of what I look like from a professional angle:

> **James F. is a fun loving person with a very active social life and numerous close friends. He often organizes trips, dinners, and parties that include his friends and relatives. He enjoys dining well, is a wine connoisseur and an excellent cook. He is well liked by his students and highly regarded by his peers. He is an avid world traveler and readily adapts to new situations. James F. claims he has never been deeply depressed and hates to go to sleep because he is**

"afraid he is going to miss something." As a result he sleeps only 4–5 hours per night, often partying and drinking until 1 or 2 in the morning and rising at 6AM. He states that his childhood asthma problem gave him a sense of his own mortality and, at a young age, he decided to live life to the fullest. This was enhanced by decades of over 700 panic attacks that started when he was 18 years old. I should point out that he has run one of the largest amateur NFL football betting pools in the nation, something he does for pleasure rather than money. Although he has been going to the race-track since he was three years old and to Las Vegas to gamble and party for decades, he bets only small sums of money, is not a compulsive gambler. He writes screenplays for fun, and all in all, he and his family live a comfortable life style . . .

James F.'s IQ scores are in the very superior range, similar to his scores in different tests in the past (IQ scores in the 150s). He showed very balanced verbal and performance cerebral functioning. (Notes—L and K [lie scale and defensiveness scale] values suggest he wants to present himself in an idealized manner, shows good ego strength, emotional defensiveness, good contact with reality, a perfectionist, excellent coping skills, but potentially poor introspection.) His clinical scores suggest a pattern of 1) adaptability, 2) decisiveness, 3) a secure self image, 4) a good natured optimistic disposition with low psychological stress, 5) independence, 6) assertiveness, 7) robust energy levels, 8) alertness, 9) an outgoing personality, 10) a high degree of self confidence, 11) sociability, and 12) spontaneity. The scores also indicate that he approaches the world in a balanced, if somewhat "Marlboro Man" type manner. His scores also intimate verbal fluency, a high level of gregariousness with a degree of hyperactivity. This may also reflect a concern for power, recognition, and status. All of these putative personal qualities have been corroborated by a decade of close personal observation of the subject by one of the interviewers as well as by the results of the other tests . . . He is a very ambitious hard working academician who has had a fulfilling, successful career while enjoying a hedonistic life style. Thus, in spite of a hypothetical lack of true insight, he has developed a high degree of coping skills necessary to achieve his career goals, although his scores hint at self-centeredness and possible difficulty in getting close to others.

Possible impulsivity, self-reliance, women not always shown in a sympathetic light, MMPI [Minnesota Multiphasic Personality Inventory] indicates James F. reveals little of his inner self, TAT [Thematic Apperception Test] scores suggest strong father figure but lack of mother image in stories, no response to homosexuality, sexually normal definitely not a prude. HTP [House-Tree-Person test] drawings suggest infantile egocentrism and body narcissism. Easily adapts, is an extratensive social butterfly, interacts well in other cultures, extensive social and professional network.

Suggests narcissistic tendencies of grandiosity and self-preoccupation, human responses pure to others perhaps at a superficial level, highly positive estimate of self worth, could strive beyond his capabilities. Some tests show superficial relationships to others, and manipulative, but not in a destructive way. He lives a very high stress life style but appears to have sufficient psychological resources to deal with it. He did exhibit some grandiosity and narcissism as well as some unmet dependency needs but these may not be significant.

I didn't disagree with the findings but laughed off the negative aspects, as I do with everything.

None of the psychological tests I took prior to 2006 addressed the issue of psychopathy directly. And since there is no formal definition of a psychopath, no formal test was going to be able to determine whether I was one. In retrospect, however, the assessments did point out several traits that are common in psychopaths—grandiosity, narcissism, egocentricity, thrill-seeking, dependency, a potential for poor self-assessment, and superficiality in relationships—a point I had never considered in the context of psychopathy. These somewhat egotistical, "blowhard," devil-may-care traits were of no real matter to me, because I wasn't antisocial.

Soon after Oslo I also remembered two long and emotionally charged letters that I had received within the same year, 2000, from people very near and dear to me. The letters were from two of the most important women in my life—my sister, Carol, and my daughter Shannon. They had not talked to each other about these letters before sending them and only found out about the other's in late 2012, after I told them. Both letters expressed extreme disappointment in the way I treated them over the years. Both intimated that I was shallow and, too often, untrustworthy. At the heart of these letters was their feeling that they had given me all their trust, emotion, support, and love over our lifetimes, but that I gave almost nothing back. I returned nothing to them in terms of deep connection or real, interpersonal, emotional empathy, the kind of empathy people cherish and need most.

My sister and I had been close growing up, and I protected her, but I'd been drifting off over the years without realizing it. Carol didn't mention any specific episode but said she always has to ask for affection. Imagine being a friend with someone for thirty years and realizing you always initiate contact, asking, "How are you? Is everything all right?" without the favor being returned. My sister always initiated the contact and caring, and the sum total finally got to her.

Unlike my sister's, I think my daughter's letter was triggered by one incident, although it was backed by years of pain. The whole family was planning to go out to a holiday dinner. I had been up partying the night before, so when they were leaving the house, I told them I'd meet them at the restaurant a little later. Shannon opted to leave her youngest son at home with me, and I said I'd bring him with me when I came. But I forgot my grandson was there in bed and showed up at the restaurant without him. My daughter felt like I didn't care enough to worry about him or re-member him—my own grandson.

When I received the letters, I thought, "What did I do to deserve this?" I didn't get it. With my sister I thought, "What am I supposed to do? I'm busy. I've got a family. If I can't give you enough, that's just too bad. I'll be supportive, but I'm not going to be someone who gives you that call." I figured it's unfortunate if I can't give people enough of what they want, but that's just who I am. In the end I just concluded that my sister and daughter must be unhappy about something else in their lives, and that they were taking out that unhappiness on me.

These letters bothered me, but not enough to change my behavior. It took me a decade to put the messages of the two letters together and take them seriously. When I pulled the letters out of my archives and read them again, however, they depressed me for several days. I was able to shake off the brunt of guilt, but not completely. When I told Carol and Shannon that I had reread them and had finally seen what the letters meant, and that I understood how I must have hurt them, they both told me not to worry about it. In a way, I still have not had what could be described as full closure about this correspondence, or the underlying issues that motivated Shannon and Carol to write the letters, but they insisted they had come to an understanding that I just am who I am and that, for them, the case was closed. I don't believe that for a second. I think they were just being nice.

After a year of hearing what my family and colleagues thought of me, I said to myself for the first time in my life, "What the hell have I done?" I wasn't despairing, just coming to terms with my cluelessness. All these pieces of the puzzle over the decades were snapping into place. About three minutes later another, different feeling took over. And with all the honesty I am capable of, I admitted to myself, "I don't care." That's right, "I DON'T CARE." At that moment, I realized for the first time in my life that what they had all been intimating, then whispering, then yelling to me all along, for all those years, was true.

After my "condition" became public in 2011 through TV and radio appearances, there was not a noticeable difference in the way most people treated me. Most people, including Diane and some of my other family members and friends, just told me, "I'm not surprised to hear you have some sociopathy in you, not surprised at all."

But once this all came out, Susannah, one of my first postdoc researchers, who used to go on trips with me all the time for work, said she didn't want to be alone with me anymore. She and her husband, Mark, will still ask me over to their house all the time, but they want to be with the animal only when he's in a social cage. They don't think I'm violent, but they worry I'll manipulate them into situations they'll regret if left to their own defenses.

One other close friend, Mary Beth, a younger woman I've written a couple of papers with, told me straight up, "You're a psychopath and I don't want to be around you anymore." She has left my life, apparently for good, even though we had always had a good relationship. We'd never fought and I can't think of any incident that would have driven her away. She's a trained Wiccan, and I guess she saw too much darkness in me, like that priest who said I was evil. It's too bad, because she was fun and interesting to be around. Diane liked her, too. I miss her honesty the most. When she said something it was absolutely truthful, which meant she often said some unpleasant things. That's such a hard quality to find in people. So I miss her, but that's the way it goes.

In contrast to Susannah and Mary Beth, other people didn't change their behavior around me at all. Surprisingly about forty friends and acquaintances wanted to spend much more time with me than ever before. I suppose some of them may have just been curious about their "special" friend. Even I can enjoy some of that gallows humor over my own condition.

So the net effect is that more people want to be around me, but I lost a few close friends. Which would you rather have? It's an acid test. Honestly, in a way I'd rather have the superficial relationships—the more the merrier. I know that's not right. I can monitor what's right and wrong, but I don't feel it and I don't care about it, and it doesn't change my behavior.

One area of concern was how this whole "outing" would affect my relationships with professional colleagues. It turns out that since many of them had already seen through me over the years and had accepted my behavior, they treated me as they had before, occasionally pausing to give me a good ribbing over it. I'm still being asked to review journal articles for publication, to be a co-investigator on grants, and to give scientific talks, so perhaps my professional standing will survive all of this. But I'm sure an important aspect of this acceptance is that I've never been accused of professional misconduct, or inappropriate behavior with students or staff or other personnel with whom I've worked. Above and beyond this, my colleagues have been wonderfully supportive and good-natured about my coming out.

Fabio, one of my closest colleagues—and friends—knows all my warts and still enjoys working with me. He sees me as a functionally flawed person and finds that interesting. He's an extremely empathetic person—my opposite—and knows my lack of feeling, but I've always helped him, and he knows I'd never intentionally betray him. And we have fun together and share a lot of interests—food, wine, travel—as well as a sense of scientific adventure. He trusts me with personal information, but he doesn't trust me to always do what I'm expected to do workwise (I blow things off sometimes), and when it's playtime he knows when not to get involved.

I sat down recently with my close friend Leonard, a psychiatrist who knows just about everything about me, to ask him what my most chronic psychopathic behaviors are. He agreed that my willingness to skip an uncle's funeral, a friend's wedding, a graduation, a bar mitzvah, First Communion, or wake certainly qualifies me as a Psychopath Lite. I don't murder people at these events; I simply don't go if I find out about another party or activity that stokes my interest more.

He also agreed that my willingness, eagerness really, to put friends and family in serious danger, just so I might "share" an exciting time, would qualify as a psychopathic trait. I asked him if all of my physical and social risk-taking is just an expression of my sense of adventure. He said that might be true, but my wanton lack of concern for the safety of others while partaking in these adventures puts my endangerment of them far outside the realm of normal behavior.

I then asked him if my drinking binges might be a cause of my abnormal behaviors. He reminded me that I'm universally known as a fun and benevolent drunk, and that is true. If I've been drinking, my empathy for everyone, even and perhaps especially strangers, goes up a notch. And to this day, alcohol is my only drug of abuse, even though a day doesn't go by that I don't pine for a cigarette.

He and I went forward to test other waters. He knows of some things that I have done that I will not discuss here, and some things I am taking to my grave. But there was one type of behavior that really bothered him that I can relate here.

I asked him if revenge counts as a psychopathic trait. He said everyone is driven to seek revenge of some sort. It is normal to get angry when someone wrongs you, and to confront the other person and even to demand retribution. He asked me to describe how I get angry with someone, and how I might seek revenge.

I told him that when someone gets me mad, I can immediately suppress the anger. Unless someone knows me intimately, they will not realize I'm mad, perhaps even furious with them. I am a master of suppressing the expression of anger or a look of revenge. And I can delay revenge for years. But at some point, when that person least expects it, I get even. People have wronged me in business or professionally or personally, and I've gotten them in the end. For me, it's fun because they don't realize what's happened. (I can't give details because I got some people really good.) I'm careful to measure the revenge proportional to the original offense to me, and not one iota more or less. And I have no interest in physically harming anyone.

My explanation clearly shocked my psychiatrist friend. And he said I related this trait to him in such a cold-blooded way that it made him shake. This ability to strategically delay revenge, he told me, was my most psychopathic trait. I told him I do other things, and these were worse behaviors, but he just waved his hand to my face and said, "That's okay, Jim, you needn't tell me any more."

I started to ask myself if other aspects of my behavior mitigate my psychopathic traits. When I asked myself the question in this way, I was quick to justify my actions. It reminded me of when I used to go to confession to reveal my sins. I realized at this point in my life that such attempts at making peace with a deity, or my own soul, on a weekly or monthly or yearly basis was a rather pathetic attempt to deny my psychopathy, as if each time I could wash my sins away just by admitting to them and asking myself or a cleric or God for forgiveness. I knew these acts of confession and contrition and seeking of grace would not change my behaviors, but were only performed to make excuses for them. If a sinner, like any psychopath, is anything, he or she is a repeat offender. We are machines and cannot fundamentally change ourselves through sheer force of will.

I considered that I could change myself superficially by simply changing the narrative story line of my behaviors. Maybe, by altering the words and definitions, the psychopathy could be made more tolerable, even lovable, if the story were crafted well enough. I could be like someone who describes himself as having a refreshing, flexible, open, and healthy attitude to sex, rather than just admitting to himelf that what he really is is promiscuous. But that wouldn't alter any of the underlying behavior. So to see myself for who I am, and then maybe even try to change for the better, I would need a plan of behavioral redemption. But the inherent problem I could not shake is that, try as I may, I really just don't care. There it is again. I do have some desire to keep the people around me happy, but that's mostly because it makes my own life easier and more pleasant.

Where does this leave the people close to me? In 2011, I was invited to give a Moth talk as part of the World Science Festival. The Moth is a storytelling and radio series in which people from all walks of life tell a story about their lives. The stories are usually personal, and often funny, so I took it as an opportunity. I can't stand giving the same talk over and over again and wanted to say something different from what I'd said in previous talks. I got my genetics work done for the *Wall Street Journal* article because I wanted to say something new, and this Moth story needed a good ending. So I decided to try to change my behavior, to actually go to the funerals and the weddings and the visits to the hospitals and sickbeds and devastatingly tedious lunches with a friend in need, offering some emotional support, an ear of empathy, if you will.

I also saw the attempt to change my behavior as an experiment or a challenge. I am a scientist, after all. Can I try to be better behaved and act more empathetic even though I don't care? It was a competition with myself, and every time I succeeded at doing the "right" thing, my hypothesis was proven correct. That's a mechanistic, frivolous sort of thing, but I still cared about it. Plus, I figured I probably owed it to the people around me. So there were three reasons to change.

And I actually started to do these things as opposed to going to the parties, the racetrack, the casino, the funky dives with inappropriate companions, playing out outrageous acts of senseless bravado and danger, and I have continued to do them to this day. But honestly . . . my heart really isn't in it. It was more of a game of whether I could do it, and it continues to be that. I figured, however, that just doing these simple humane and human things instead of feeding my amygdala and hedonism circuits might even temporarily strengthen some weak synaptic circuitry so that I could re-habit my habits into behaviors more suitable to a mensch than a psychopath. And it seems to be working a little.

The people around me, especially those close to me, notice these little differences. And they don't mind too much that my heart isn't really in it the way a normal person's would be. True, there may be some phoniness to all of this, but people seem to appreciate that I'm trying, that for some reason I'm exerting that effort and eschewing the wild times in order to be with them, and treat them with more respect, like a good companion should.

But I can see some troubles brewing with all this Boy Scout

stuff. There is a whole repertoire of things I do that are not im-moral, or unethical, yet are most assuredly inappropriate, like getting another professor to dance on a table, drunk at a bar. At least that is what I'm told by the people I'm being inappropriate with. But I don't get it. If what I'm doing is not wrong in any fun-damental way, who cares? Well, here is the rub. People could, again as I am told, take things the wrong way, and that will hurt them. At the same time, I really don't know if I'll be able to give up those morally neutral but apparently inappropriate behaviors. Like many people, I was able to stop smoking, cold turkey, after decades of heavy smoking, and have not smoked a whiff since 1998. I've been able to lose from sixty to a hundred pounds eight times (only to gain it back, of course). But changing the really big, interpersonal stuff? No.

As I write, I've been able to go into long-term social isolation from all the hedonism I love so dearly, the heavy drinking and eating and partying and gambling and Internet surfing and TV watching and going absolutely wild on a regular basis. But I'm learning something: the substances and the activities are not what I'm craving at all. It is the buzz from the social interactions that go with these activities that I'm "addicted" to. Frankly, I find most people uninteresting and boring, but under those circumstances of wildness, they all seem wonderful. These excessive and danger-ous activities must be about getting a replacement for those hu-man connections, the simple and pure and natural buzz of empathy and togetherness others must experience. So far I'm close to tolerating the shift and to sometimes even enjoying the company of others in a safe and sane and sober and clothed environment. But there are only a handful of times when the simple pleasure of having a glass of water and hanging out with someone has been enjoyable. There are a few people, mostly family members, with whom that has always been true. But beyond that, no.

I've written part of this book at my friend Larry's cabin in the San Bernardino Mountains, and part at Fabio's father's house in a medieval town overlooking Lago d'Orta in Italy. Living a monastic, sedentary lifestyle with little coffee or alcohol, I don't wheeze or get acid reflux as much anymore, and I've stopped most of the heroic, mind-blowing snoring, at least temporarily. I'm now sleeping five hours a night instead of four, but to me that is not such a good thing. I get plenty done in my extra hours of wakefulness. That has helped my career, helped me win at everything except, of course, the fight against a fifty-inch waistline. But there are some undeniably negative things that are also occurring. I rarely got sick after I was a toddler. Now I'm getting lumps and rashes and aches and pains I never had before. This may be due to the toxins accrued in fat from years of self-abuse of all types, now being released into my tissues, and believe me, it isn't fun or pretty.

Which gets me back to the main challenge I face. At what point do I stop being "good"? I've always liked myself and still do, and have absolutely enjoyed my whole life to this point, and things seem to be getting better as the decades go by. All the maladies and near-maladies I've had over the years just seem to have made me tougher and happier. I want to keep it that way, and the moment I start to become unhappy in order to make anyone else happy is the moment I put on the brakes. I don't want to have to give up all those inappropriate and dangerous activities with inappropriate people, even those that happen to put others close to me in life-threatening, career-ending harm's way. I do love that so, and that will be my bright line in the sand.

As far as "will" is concerned, I want someone to say with a straight face that Oprah, with her constant losing battles against obesity, lacks will. That woman has more will than 99.9 percent of people. But it is not the "will" that society, her friends, her family want. They want her to be wonderful and to do great works, and be famous, *and* be thin. Well, folks, unless she gives up everything else and stays focused solely on her weight for the rest of her life, she is going to keep coming back home. All behaviors can be modified in the face of a genetic and epigenetic makeup that says otherwise. But to stay changed in the face of those genetic imperatives usually means you have to give up nearly everything else you hold most dear. Our genes and how their effects are modified by stressful experiences early in life don't necessarily predict categorically who we are and what our deep character is about, but they create constant pressures to be and act a certain way.

Psychopathic tendencies are particularly hard to fight, and attempted cures may make only small differences. Drugs that influence the monoamine neurotransmitter systems can partially reduce impulsivity and aggression, and early interventions involving diet and meditation can decrease behavioral problems, but the core neuropsychological deficits leading to lack of empathy and remorse remain. There are no magic bullets.

I'll continue to ignore the most basic rules of proper social conduct, and anything a government or church control freak decides is good for us. Social structures like religion allow you to wash yourselves of your sociopathic behaviors, atone, and be absolved and start over fresh and pure. I used to call my bad behaviors sins. Now I'm just calling them psychopathic behaviors, something I won't get rid of or feel guilty about ever again.

When I see a sign directing me to park somewhere proper and legal, whether for a restaurant or sports event, I will continue to ignore the rules, knowing that the sign is there to serve whoever put up the sign, and not the rest of us. I'll find a place on the grass or next to a real space close to the door, partly because I'm lazy and partly because I like getting away with it. While these scofflaw behaviors are not really psychopathic in any serious sense, they do signify I can be a real jerk, or, as less polite people may call me, an asshole.

The diagnosis of psychopathy is culturally dependent to some degree. Rules are usually created for someone else's comfort and peace of mind. And yes, I do know that I am missing a few screws when it comes to knowing right from wrong in social matters. I don't think I've ever understood morality anyway. As an obsessed child and hyper-religious young teen I was feeding a need for order. I didn't get morality then, and may not get it now, fifty years later. But what the hell, I'll give it a try just out of curiosity if nothing else.

I guess there are several ways I can go from here. Perhaps a place to start is to try to treat the people closest to me better, to show up at the weddings and funerals and birthday parties even if I have to feign enthusiasm. Maybe enough practice doing the good and right things will recondition my taste for fun and pleasure, and I suspect that might take a year or three to get used to. I can report to you now that when I do something for Diane or with her that I wouldn't have before, or go the little extra step to help her or notice her when I wouldn't before, she seems to like it, and honestly, that is a buzz for me now.

Any behavioral improvements on my part, however, have to start happening sooner rather than later. I have too many friends who have become "good," but they know and I know without saying it that they simply can't get it up anymore, "it," of course, referring to that little creature in our limbic system that whispers for us to beat the boredom and take that little peek outside the pigsty that might tempt us now and then. While some people may be able to change some of their behaviors through concerted attempts, those behaviors that are most deeply driven from the genetic machinery, whether they be addictive behavior or a lack of empathy, are something else. I can change my behaviors like others can, but, like others, the main destructive habits always return a year or ten later. Even psychopathic serial killers can go for years without succumbing to the drive to murder, but at some point the urge overpowers all other priorities. My urges are much less destructive than that, fortunately, and if I make it my priority above all other concerns, they may be tamed.

I need to see my innocent teasing and practical jokes for the hurt that they can cause. Even though unintentionally bothersome, these behaviors fringe on sadism, the more I look at them and their effects on the happiness of others.

Recently my mother told me, "Jim, I know you better than anyone, and deep down there somewhere is a sensitive, good guy." That may be the good guy she knew from the early years, before my prefrontal cortex switched to a full cognitive mode, leaving emotional empathy and even some morality in the dust. I remember that little boy and young teenager who collected all the sacks of Halloween candy to drop them off at midnight at the doorsteps of charities, but that little boy is someone or somewhere else now.

I sometimes have to remind myself about the things I've been doing since that little boy grew up that were good and perhaps useful to others. I never lost my general connection to strangers. I continue to try to help people in trouble who contact me out of the blue. And I'll continue not to ask for money or thanks or anything in return, perhaps as a tip of the hat to my father and uncle and father-in-law, who gave so generously to strangers, and anonymously. Although I do not believe in real altruism—everything we do is at least a little bit selfish—their behavior has approached that ideal.

I've tried to remember some of the consistent behaviors that I should probably keep. I realize that my idea of ethics and morality is probably different from that of most people. To me ethics are a set of rules governing behavior that are specific to a group or a society. The prefrontal cortex learns them and then teaches them to the ventromedial and orbital cortex. But morality is inherent. Kids don't need to be taught murder is wrong. My morals aren't so good, but I do have some sense of ethics. For example, one time in grad school, long after I'd shed my persona as Catholic Boy of the Year, I saw the questions for an upcoming final exam on a secretary's desk and refused to take the test, reporting that I would have an unfair advantage since I knew the questions. Okay, I stole some cars with friends when I was younger, but we didn't want to hurt people, and we returned the cars, so really it was just borrowing. Occasionally I got involved in frisky adolescent behaviors like breaking into houses with friends and drinking the booze we found there. But that was lightweight childhood stuff and I knew it wasn't right.

Another ethical quandary came up in the early 1990s, when Diane asked, given our political beliefs against a large federal government and its grants and aids programs, whether I could accept federally funded grants. Private grants, even state grants, would be fine, but because I oppose federal taxation to support education and research, I couldn't in good conscience continue to be funded in this way. We knew this would affect some significant percentage of our income up to about 35 percent, our level of pension funding, and my promotions. But there it was, and it had to be done. To that point, I had enjoyed fifteen years of federal grant funds, but I stopped taking them. I've softened on the issue because categorically refusing federal money would have inhibited good work in my lab, which seemed silly. I said I'll take money but not be primary investigator on grants. To some that's a cop-out, but I want to be practical. We're always dealing with contradiction and struggling to find a sensible, sane way to deal with problems.

So I believe I do have some personal sense of ethics and morality, regardless of how others might see it.

There is still a significant amount of unfinished business in my life and, more important, in my relationships. This point was driven home as I added the final touches to this book in the spring of 2013. I wanted to include some recent genetic findings on a potential link between mood, obesity, sleep, panic, anxiety, and psychopathy. I e-mailed Diane a rough draft of this material, and she responded later that night, "I don't know how you can say you haven't been able to figure out why the swings in weight occur. They occur because you don't move—and don't sleep . . . You don't want to do it and that's fine, actually. You don't need to make excuses. This is how you choose to live, period. I think you would be more honest with yourself (and everyone else) if you simply say, 'I hate any kind of physical exercise and I'd prefer obesity to exercise.'"

Her response irked me. I was disappointed that after everything I'd taught her about genetics, physiology, and medicine she wouldn't accept the biological explanations for my list of lousy behaviors. Then I stepped back and realized that my ire was indicative of something still way off in me. She was trying to be perfectly candid and helpful and was crying out for me to just snap out of my perceptual blindness.

From my earliest years, when I suffered from severe asthma, I have associated exercise with an inability to breathe. But after I started taking medication for the asthma as a young adult, I could control the onset, and the fear of the asthma attacks, just as I had

learned to control my panic attacks in my late twenties and thirties. So I didn't really have an excuse not to exercise, and Diane
was right. I'm not a kid anymore, but I continue to act like one.
Nonetheless, I still absolutely hate to exercise. But when this book
is done, I will try to swim several times a week and walk again.
This is the least I can do for her, and me, and our grandchildren.

CHAPTER 10

Why Do Psychopaths Exist?

Do we need psychopaths? This may be a leading question. Do we need saints, or rock stars, or people who do no evil but do no good, either? Such questions can quickly turn into a goofy parlor game, but there may be meaning in addressing them. Scientists tend not to phrase things in such a way, nor do they ask if and why evolution creates and sculpts species. The commonsense approach may be to wonder why evolution was created, or why species were created, but this is upside-down thinking or, more directly, magical thinking, religious thinking, which may be useful sometimes, but not for scientists. Instead of looking for inherent purposes to behaviors in a universal master plan, scientists tend to say: What conditions were present that allowed for certain realities to come about, certain genes associated with certain traits to survive and thrive? Put more succinctly, what evolutionary survival advantage do such traits, and the genes that underlie them, offer?

Psychopaths are present in all human societies. The pancultural reality of psychopathy, at a rate of about 2 percent, suggests that psychopathy, or at least the traits and associated alleles found in psychopaths, is somehow "desirable" in humanity. Otherwise evolution should have wiped them out or at least diminished their numbers ages ago. You might think that because brain damage and childhood abuse also contribute (according to my Three-Legged Stool theory), psychopathy is just an unfortunate outcome of these negative environmental effects. But those effects have always been there throughout evolution—parents have always beat or abandoned their kids—and the genes contributing to psycho-pathy have persisted given those real-world conditions, so maybe they and their associated psychopathic traits contribute some sur-vival advantage.

Perhaps full psychopaths, those scoring 30 points or more on the Hare Checklist, are just a statistical fluke or a roll of the dice in the genetic casino, amassing too many of the genes that are helpful individually. But 2 percent is a lot of people. And that number is constant across races, even though the prevalence of specific genes, such as the warrior gene, vary widely. We should consider why psychopathic traits might be individually advanta-geous, or at least tolerable, from an evolutionary standpoint.

There has been a concerted effort by some behaviorists in the past decade or so to argue that the natural state of human inter-action is one of peace, harmony, altruism, and eleemosynary be-havior. While some humans do exhibit seeming holiness, the bulk of human history is highlighted by recurrent mayhem, cruelty, greed, and war. So other neuroscientists support the notion that humans are basically selfish, greedy, and violent, even when their outward behavior seems sweet, giving, and peaceful. Many people wear masks so they can just get on with life and be liked, accepted, and loved. Few want to be shunned by society. This also allows us to selfishly pursue sex and resources at the expense of others, ultimately helping our genes. If your intentions are no good, hiding them helps you get what you desire, and prevents you from being booted from the community and the gene pool.

Most people with a conscience have tells that betray their thoughts and emotions. That's why most people are poor poker players. But psychopaths are masters at hiding their true intentions. One of their disarming but pernicious attributes is their ability to remain cool when they lie.

Since psychopaths don't feel emotion the way normal humans do, they don't give the same tells as others. Because their ability for cold cognition is so much greater than their ability for hot, emotional cognition, true functioning (or successful) psychopaths can dream up fantastic lies and never show any sign of guilt or remorse. Some psychopaths do respond emotionally, as measured by heart rate and galvanic skin response, and these sorts, mostly men, can be ferreted out faster. And, of course, there are cases of psychopaths who are prone to acting impulsively when faced with stress or anxiety, for instance when caught in an act of treachery. These people are, at least, less dangerous because they're easier to spot.

Psychopaths also benefit in other ways from their lack of anxiety. The steroid hormone cortisol, the body's main stress hormone, travels throughout the body to carry out parts of the stress response, including the mobilization of sugar, fat, and protein metabolism, and an inhibition of the immune system. Thus, under constant stress, the body is less able to fight disease. People who naturally have little stress, such as psychopaths, can avoid most diseases their whole lives because their immune system is always working at peak efficiency.

So, in theory, a psychopath could live a nice, healthy, long life of manipulating people to get what he wants without anyone cottoning on. Charming.

Even known psychopaths don't have trouble finding mates. You'll always find women waiting outside prisons for murderers to come out. Psychopaths can be great at showering affection on partners, who often want to be lied to. Many people are looking for the unconditional love and devotion that a psychopath can fake—at some point a regular person would say, "Listen, babe, I'm not going to put up with your crap." The attention can be like a drug for women, and they put up with a certain amount of pain to get that buzz.

Family members, especially mothers and wives, will tolerate psychopaths because they look for some spark of empathy and think they can change the person. Of course, the person never changes. It's like a guy who marries a girl he met at an orgy and then is surprised when two years later she's sleeping with somebody else. Even smart people can fool themselves in that way. Everyone wants to think they can control another person's behavior and destiny: "I have a special relationship with him and I can see the good in him. I know he's a good boy." Psychopaths know how to make people feel special. They can draw them in, hook them, and then, in some cases, the beatings and humiliation start, followed by, "I love you." The family member will say, "He can't help himself. I know he's got an animal inside, but I can deal with him." So the wife and mother protect him. For brothers and other family members, there's a sense of loyalty, an empathy toward the clan. So even as a psychopath makes enemies, his blood stands by him.

How should you behave around someone you know to be a full psychopath? Do not appear to be vulnerable in any way. If it's a brief encounter, don't engage. Just smile and walk away. At every party with a hundred people, there's probably a psychopath in there, and he's looking for weakness. If it's an ongoing interaction, watch the person carefully and keep track of any odd behavior. Psychopaths will navigate their way through an office or a friend group, always looking for alliances. They may know you're not vulnerable but will use little pieces of information about you to gain leverage with others. It's a chess game. They'll play a whole group, looking for one or two vulnerable people they can use to obtain whatever they're looking for, whether it's sex or money or power. So they'll observe their target's interactions and prepare to deal with a suspicious sister or office manager. Then they'll try to engage with those people and neutralize them by seeming like a nice guy. There are a lot of secondary and tertiary characters to utilize even just a little bit. How do you protect against that? Tell people that this guy might try to con you. But be careful. Don't make a big deal, or he might get even with you. And you won't know how he'll do it.

Clearly individuals can benefit if they have psychopathic tendencies, but what about society as a whole? Do psychopaths have anything to offer the rest of us?

They can be strong leaders. A recent study from Caltech found that people with the warrior gene make better financial decisions under risk. Whereas many people will freeze in a stressful situation, real leaders take chances, as do psychopaths. In a position of power, they'll branch out into new markets when times are uncertain, or they'll activate the military or take their tribe over the next mountain. This may work out for the group they're in charge of, or it may not. On a larger scale, it benefits civilization to have groups take chances, because some will succeed and move civilization forward—just as biological evolution benefits from mutations, even though many of them are deadly.

We also need individuals with narcissism, because to have the energy to be a leader you've got to be full of yourself. Who the hell else would want to be a president or CEO if they really knew what it involved? You need heavy egotism and a lot of glibness and a bit of bullshit to aspire to that kind of work and to do it well.

Robert Hare, the man behind the psychopath checklist, sees psychopathy at work in the finance and banking and investment community, perhaps in some people like Bernie Madoff. (A strong study showing greater psychopathy in business hasn't been done, but the hypothesis is reasonable.) It could be argued that the only reason these money-managing swindlers exist is that the general public wants to make that quick and easy buck and, while lacking their own combination of high risk and knowledge, use hired guns like Madoff and other investment mavens to do their dirty work for them. The person most effective in making you money will often be a little bit psychopathic, because he's not there to save the world. Of course, there are plenty of problems with relying on these guys. They can be found out—like Madoff was—or, when push comes to shove, they will turn out to have benefited at your expense. Nonetheless, common experience tells us that many of us love hot merchandise, we love a tough and heartless CEO, and we love tough guys who make us money and protect us.

It could easily be argued that we all have a bit of larceny in our souls, and we welcome the employ of clever and ruthless psychopaths to get us what we want. At some point, don't most people wish they could have their own mafia to mete out justice? Haven't you harbored thoughts about seeking revenge or playing dirty to get ahead? The top business executives I know, leaders of Fortune 500 companies, are not psychopaths at all. They're family men who are good to their underlings. But I've worked with some CEOs of smaller companies who are psychopaths—maybe it's easier to get away with this at a private versus public company. I know one investment counselor who was effective and ruthless in his work. But he took his quirk to the outer limits. He even boasted that in trying to get another guy's girlfriend, he created a situation where the guy ended up committing suicide. This is a gentleman who is hard to like or admire in any way.

Kent Kiehl, a noted expert on psychopathy and especially the brains of criminal psychopaths, has estimated that the national cost of criminal psychopathy per year, in 2011 dollars, is $460 billion, an order of magnitude greater than the cost of depression. That covers prosecution, incarceration, and damages, but if it were possible to add in the costs of nonviolent psychopathy, the numbers would potentially be staggering. Are there advantages to psychopathy that actually save money? One could make the case that *Dexter*-style justice saves the economy billions, in that psychopaths can mete out justice at very low societal costs. Don't the Mafia and the gangs tend to kill their own? A psychopathic gang leader can limit violence by being surgical rather than explosive. They don't want to be caught, they don't want their business to be screwed up, and they don't want other people seeking revenge against them for an unjust wrong. This is a tough argument to swallow, but if we are just talking economics, psychopaths may actually save society money on one end of their behavioral spectrum while they are burning it on the other.

Psychopaths also make strong warriors. Humans love to go to war, or at least they deem it necessary, seeing as we've been killing each other in the name of survival since our species came into being. It's pointless to deny the existence of these instincts, no matter how you feel about war itself. Supporting war doesn't necessarily make one psychopathic; humans will do anything to preserve themselves, even break the law or kill if they need to. That's normal behavior, and Western society doesn't consider that immoral.

Modern humans are much less violent, in terms of per capita killing rates in battle, than our ancestors. Australopithecine hominid warriors, three to four million years ago, appear to have been the most effective killers, and over the eons, modern humans have been maiming and killing at lower and lower rates so that now, in the early twenty-first century, we have the least lethal human civilization of all time. Part of this "savings" may be due to the development of more effective long-range weaponry, as we have transited from clubs to spears to artillery to ICBMs and now drones. Impersonal and devastating distance weaponry may have created the necessity of more effective alliances to keep war at bay. Otherwise, all-out warfare could be catastrophic. I also point out to my horrified friends (when I offer such apologia) that the people I know in the military are the most antiwar people I've come across because they understand the full cost of battle. (A few, as might be expected, rather enjoy war, much as prizefighters or even some street fighters just live to fight, a phenomenon found in my own extended family to a surprising degree.)

The most successful warriors and fighters appear to be those who disengage emotionally from the action. In battle, soldiers try to take out people methodically, without being scared to pull the trigger and without getting pleasure from it. A soldier has to be able to determine the real target and go for it without prejudice or emotion. In regular society that could be considered psychopathic, but in warfare it's very useful, where fifty milliseconds is the difference between life and death.

And psychopaths have a better chance of surviving the battle once they've returned home and have less risk of suffering PTSD. As a specialist on cognition and war, I advise some military think tanks and am working with colleagues to find ways to maximize the effectiveness of soldiers while simultaneously reducing the risk that they will suffer PTSD or commit suicide. Those who are less prone to feel emotions are probably less likely to experience this sort of trauma.

The problem with inviting psychopaths to war, however, is that the military also wants soldiers to be team players who can connect with their unit and fight not only against the enemy but *for* their own.

Retired colonel Jack Pryor, an experienced warrior and a regular family guy, told me he can naturally turn on or off his fighting instinct. His last fight in Vietnam was a massacre. He and another guy, after their assassination mission, were yanked out in a chopper and taken back to Da Nang before flying home to San Francisco. He said he was having a meal on the plane and looked down and saw brain and blood all over him. This is a guy who can assassinate someone and then go have a burger, but he's not a psychopath.

Can such an effective emotionality on-off switch be found in fighters other than Royce Gracie and Jack, and applied to the recruitment and training of combat personnel? This can be determined, but probably at a cost of hundreds of millions of dollars in long-term research. One option is to artificially flip the switch using transcranial magnetic stimulation (TMS). If you put a focused electromagnetic coil in the helmet you might be able to disrupt emotionality at the flip of a literal switch. Off: social mode. On: killer mode.

Often women will say that there is something adorable, attractive, and sexy about bad boys. The problem is that what is sexually attractive to a girl of mating age may later become the reason she wants a divorce. Some of us may, from time to time, want our own personal enforcer we can ultimately control and call our own. In a sense many of us ask for psychopaths, as absurd as this sounds. Some of us may want the excitement, the dangerous mayhem that psychopaths can offer. The near-lovable psychopath has almost become a romantic hero in our popular culture, from Robert De Niro in *Analyze This*, to Joe Pesci in *Goodfellas*, to Heath Ledger in *The Dark Knight*. Perhaps being able to fear and love these characters in a controlled, two-dimensional film environment helps us deal with the true terror of it all.

And sometimes we want a taste of that recklessness in our own lives. There is a deliciously wicked part of us that wants to be a tiger for a day. Maybe an old maid who's been good all her life wants to have that one super-wild fling so she can feel she's lived her life fully. People want to break away from the routine of safety, social or otherwise, so they can say they did it, like the person who climbs the mountain or overcomes a fear of swimming in the ocean. They want to feel that they can push through, and when they do they feel like a lion or a tiger, someone who's ferociously independent and brave. That's one benefit of having a psychopath around. He'll afford opportunities for people to do that stuff. People tend to hang around with equally safe people. You can get a bunch of mountain climbers together, and they still have a socially safe routine. A psychopathic friend will help you get into all the trouble you want and cover up for you when you get caught. At least that's what I do.

I've already talked about how I have, on many occasions, put people in harm's way just to get a buzz. But I don't want to kill anybody or hurt anybody. And I don't like to steal things or lie. That's for losers. If you have to do that, you're a disappointment as a psychopath. Violence is crude and it destroys the fun. My concern is not moral but practical: I'm looking to get the most bang. I'm really not a badass, but if you said, "Hey, Jim, I want to drive to Mexico and get some coyotes and do this, that, and the other thing," I could get you there.

And so my friends and colleagues will ask me to take them out to dive bars. Even a sweet fifty-year-old Goody Two-shoes National Academy of Sciences member wants to have a crazy night once in a while. I might get them to dance on a table, and they might feel embarrassed, but half the time they're glad they did it.

Inherent in human genetic variability—the high dimensionality of our genome and transcriptome—is the inevitable creation of people at the far ends of the genetic and behavioral spectrum. These people may have considerable personal weaknesses, such as susceptibility to disease, but also may simultaneously have great intellectual skills. All combinations of strengths and weaknesses become manifest in humans, and this both helps and harms individuals, but also add to the group. They also add to group diversity, the ability for at least some of us to survive any extremes of plague, climate change, or total war. Within this outlying group are the psychopaths, who in peaceful times act as predators and opportunistic parasites in a society, but under times of tremendous danger may save the day and continue breeding, albeit at the cost of keeping their traits in the gene pool for as long as humans exist.

So, am I a psychopath? The categorical answer is no.

But a better answer is that I'm a prosocial psychopath. I display many of the items on the Hare Checklist, including interpersonal traits (I'm superficial, grandiose, and deceitful), affective traits (I lack remorse and empathy), and behavioral traits (I'm impulsive and irresponsible). But I'm missing the antisocial traits: I control my anger and have no criminal record. Beyond the checklist, I tend to use my powers of charm, manipulation, and hedonism for good, or at least not bad. I have fun and do good deeds, and any harm that comes is purely incidental.

Perhaps the best answer to the question, though, is that I'm a lucky psychopath. I'm lucky because of my nurturing family, with a kind and loving father and an insightful mother who saw a son in trouble early on and guided him gently. She kept her eye on me as I navigated an environment outside the family that did have its own share of bullies and predators. My avoidance of violence and abuse, coupled with the parental and extended family support and love, probably saved me. In the late winter of 2013, my mother asked me, "How long does it take to write an autobiography, for God's sake?" I had to short-circuit this line of interrogation, so I responded, "I'm not writing my autobiography, Mums, I'm writing yours." She got it immediately: this is a memoir, but a lot of who I am has to do with how she raised and treated me. My story is as much about motherhood and fatherhood and parenthood and how you raise kids as it is about me.

So I suppose the "luck" is not luck at all. It's a purposeful, nurturing environment that could be created in almost any family or neighborhood, including those seemingly destined to breed a life of underachievement, deviance, and criminality. What I discovered during this serendipitous pilgrimage beginning in my sixth decade of life is something I didn't believe in even five years ago: real nurture can overcome a lousy deck of cards dealt at birth by nature. There are good behavioral, genetic, epigenetic, psychiatric, and social reasons to clean up neighborhoods and to treat vulnerable children with an extra bit of love. It doesn't mean your kid will turn out to be perfect. I'm certainly no angel—as you've noticed if you've read this far. But I could have turned out a lot worse.

I don't think we should remove the psychopathy-related traits and genes from society. It would lead to passivity and wipe us out. We just need to identify those people with the traits early in their lives and keep them out of trouble. Individuals with low empathy and high aggression, if they're treated well, can have a positive impact. Of course, they put stress on their families and friends, as

I do, but on a macro level they're beneficial to society. Maybe this is my own narcissism speaking, but I believe there's a sweet spot on the psychopathy spectrum. People who are twenty-five or thirty on the Hare scale are dangerous, but we need a lot of twenties around—people with the chutzpah and brio and outrageousness to keep humanity vibrant and adaptable—and alive.

People like me.

ACKNOWLEDGMENTS

I'd like to thank the following people:

Miriam Goderich, who put up with my mad rantings over incomprehensible and bizarre narratives I tried to slip into the first—and then second—drafts.

Tom Stephenson, a man's man, who has such a way with words.

Matt Hutson, who made rough spots in the final draft so comprehensible.

Adrian Zackheim, my publisher, who thought my ramblings might find a wise and interested audience.

Brooke Carey, my editor, who, after a rich life of editing perfectly rational beings, has now decided to retire to the Catskills and take up the creation of artisanal cheeses.

Margot Stamas, my publicist, who had no idea what she got herself into, yet remains steadfast and vigilant on my behalf.

Katie Coe, the editorial assistant who wished I hadn't discovered that DNA profile at the bottom of the pile those years ago.

Jane Dystel, my literary agent, who embraced the psychopath but kept a wise distance.

Lawrence Lorenzi, my buddy, for the use of his cabin in Lake Arrowhead, California.

Gastone Macciardi, the father of my genetics guru, Fabio

Macciardi, for the use of his mountain retreat above Magic Mountain in Lago d'Orta, Italy.

My children Shannon (Shann), Tara (Taz), and James (never Jim!), for loving me more than I thought was humanly possible.

My grandchildren Fallon, James, Cooper, Jackson, and Chloe, for tolerating my often closed office door during their visits.

My brothers: Jack, for showing the way; Pete, for providing the energy, and then some; Tom, who took the most interesting path; and Mark, so good, balanced, and the best dancer.

My dear angelic sister, Carol, who has almost forgiven me for things I don't even know about.

My cousins Dave Bohrer and Arnie Fallon, who, over the past thirty-five years, dug up both the interesting and relevant genealogical information, and then some.

My Friend—you know who you are.

My ever supportive, riotously fun-loving, quirky, and beautiful aunts and uncles, especially Florence Scoma Irwin, my dear aunt Flo, who guided me down the path and saved me from going down the drain—the actual kitchen drain.

And Diane, the love of my life, forever.

BIBLIOGRAPHY

Aharoni, Eyal, Chadd Funk, Walter Sinnott-Armstrong, and Michael Gazzaniga. "Can neurological evidence help courts assess criminal responsibility? Lessons from law and neuroscience." *Annals of the New York Academy of Sciences* 1124, no. 1 (2008): 145–160.

Alicke, Mark D., and Olesya Govorun. "The better-than-average effect," in *The Self in Social Judgment*, ed. Mark D. Alicke et al. New York: Psychology Press, 2005, 85.

Babiak, Paul, and Robert D. Hare. *Snakes in Suits: When Psychopaths Go to Work*. New York: HarperBusiness, 2006.

Beaver, Kevin M., Matt DeLisi, Michael G. Vaughn, and J. C. Barnes. "Monoamine oxidase A genotype is associated with gang membership and weapon use." *Comprehensive Psychiatry* 51, no. 2 (2010): 130–134.

Brunner, Han G., M. Nelen, X. O. Breakefield, H. H. Ropers, and B. A. Van Oost. "Abnormal behavior associated with a point mutation in the structural gene for monoamine oxidase A." *Science* 262, no. 5133 (1993): 578–580.

Buckholtz, Joshua W., Michael T. Treadway, Ronald L. Cowan, Neil D. Woodward, Stephen D. Benning, Rui Li, M. Sib Ansari, et al. "Mesolimbic dopamine reward system hypersensitivity in individuals with psychopathic traits." *Nature Neuroscience* 13, no. 4 (2010): 419–421.

Carr, Laurie, Marco Iacoboni, Marie-Charlotte Dubeau, John C. Mazziotta, and Gian Luigi Lenzi. "Neural mechanisms of empathy in humans: A relay from neural systems for imitation to limbic areas." *Proceedings of the National Academy of Sciences* 100, no. 9 (2003): 5497–5502.

Caspi, Avshalom, Joseph McClay, Terrie E. Moffitt, Jonathan Mill, Judy Martin, Ian W. Craig, Alan Taylor, and Richie Poulton. "Role of genotype in the cycle of violence in maltreated children." *Science* 297, no. 5582 (2002): 851–854.

Chakrabarti, Bhismadev, and Simon Baron-Cohen. "Genes related to autistic traits and empathy." *From DNA to Social Cognition* (2011): 19–36.

Craddock, Nick, and Liz Forty. "Genetics of affective (mood) disorders." *European Journal of Human Genetics* 14, no. 6 (2006): 660–668.

Craig, Ian W., and Kelly E. Halton. "Genetics of human aggressive behaviour." *Human Genetics* 126, no. 1 (2009): 101–113.

Decety, Jean, Kalina J. Michalska, and Katherine D. Kinzler. "The contribution of emotion and cognition to moral sensitivity: A neurodevelopmental study." *Cerebral Cortex* 22, no. 1 (2012): 209–220.

Fallon, James H. "Neuroanatomical background to understanding the brain of the young psychopath." *Ohio State Journal of Criminal Law* 3 (2005): 341.

Fingelkurts, Alexander A., and Andrew A. Fingelkurts. "Is our brain hardwired to produce God, or is our brain hardwired to perceive God? A systematic review on the role of the brain in mediating religious experience." *Cognitive Processing* 10, no. 4 (2009): 293–326.

Forth, A. E., and F. Tobin. "Psychopathy and young offenders: Rates of childhood maltreatment." *Forum for Corrections Research*, vol. 7 (1995): 20–27.

Frydman, Cary, Colin Camerer, Peter Bossaerts, and Antonio Rangel. "MAOA-L carriers are better at making optimal financial decisions under risk." *Proceedings of the Royal Society B: Biological Sciences* 278, no. 1714 (2011): 2053–2059.

Gao, Yu, and Adrian Raine. "Successful and unsuccessful psychopaths: A neurobiological model." *Behavioral Sciences & the Law* 28, no. 2 (2010): 194–210.

Gläscher, Jan, Ralph Adolphs, Hanna Damasio, Antoine Bechara, David Rudrauf, Matthew Calamia, Lynn K. Paul, and Daniel Tranel. "Lesion mapping of cognitive control and value-based decision making in the prefrontal cortex." *Proceedings of the National Academy of Sciences* 109, no. 36 (2012): 14681–14686.

Guo, Guang, Xiao-Ming Ou, Michael Roettger, and Jean C. Shih. "The VNTR 2 repeat in MAOA and delinquent behavior in adolescence and young adulthood: Associations and MAOA promoter activity." *European Journal of Human Genetics* 16, no. 5 (2008): 626–634.

Hare, Robert D., and Hans Vertommen. *The Hare Psychopathy Checklist—Revised*. Toronto: Multi-Health Systems, 2003.

Insel, Thomas R. "The challenge of translation in social neuroscience: a review of oxytocin, vasopressin, and affiliative behavior." *Neuron* 65, no. 6 (2010): 768.

Kim-Cohen, Julia, Avshalom Caspi, Alan Taylor, Benjamin Williams, Rhiannon Newcombe, Ian W. Craig, and Terrie E. Moffitt. "MAOA, maltreatment, and gene-environment interaction predicting children's mental health: New evidence and a meta-analysis." *Molecular Psychiatry* 11, no. 10 (2006): 903–913.

Kirsch, Peter, Christine Esslinger, Qiang Chen, Daniela Mier, Stefanie Lis, Sarina Siddhanti, Harald Gruppe, Venkata S. Mattay, Bernd Gallhofer, and Andreas Meyer-Lindenberg. "Oxytocin modulates neural circuitry for social cognition and fear in humans." *The Journal of Neuroscience* 25, no. 49 (2005): 11489–11493.

Koenigs, Michael, Liane Young, Ralph Adolphs, Daniel Tranel, Fiery Cushman, Marc Hauser, and Antonio Damasio. "Damage to the prefrontal cortex increases utilitarian moral judgements." *Nature* 446, no. 7138 (2007): 908–911.

Laland, Kevin N., John Odling-Smee, and Sean Myles. "How culture shaped the human genome: Bringing genetics and the human sciences together." *Nature Reviews Genetics* 11, no. 2 (2010): 137–148.

Macdonald, John M. "The threat to kill." *American Journal of Psychiatry* 120, no. 2 (1963): 125–130.

McDermott, Rose, Dustin Tingley, Jonathan Cowden, Giovanni Frazzetto, and Dominic D. P. Johnson. "Monoamine oxidase A gene (MAOA) predicts behavioral aggression following provocation." *Proceedings of the National Academy of Sciences* 106, no. 7 (2009): 2118–2123.

McEwen, Bruce S. "Understanding the potency of stressful early life experiences on brain and body function." *Metabolism* 57 (2008): S11–S15.

Meyer-Lindenberg, Andreas, Joshua W. Buckholtz, Bhaskar Kolachana, Ahmad R. Hariri, Lukas Pezawas, Giuseppe Blasi, Ashley Wabnitz, et al. "Neural mechanisms of genetic risk for impulsivity and violence in humans." *Proceedings of the National Academy of Sciences* 103, no. 16 (2006): 6269–6274.

Murrough, James W., and Dennis S. Charney. "The serotonin transporter and emotionality: Risk, resilience, and new therapeutic opportunities." *Biological Psychiatry* 69, no. 6 (2011): 510–512.

Nordquist, Niklas, and Lars Oreland. "Serotonin, genetic variability, behaviour, and psychiatric disorders—a review." *Upsala Journal of Medical Sciences* 115, no. 1 (2010): 2–10.

Polanczyk, Guilherme, Avshalom Caspi, Benjamin Williams, Thomas S. Price, Andrea Danese, Karen Sugden, Rudolf Uher, Richie Poulton, and Terrie E. Moffitt. "Protective effect of CRHR1 gene variants on the development of adult depression following childhood maltreatment: Replication and extension." *Archives of General Psychiatry* 66, no. 9 (2009): 978.

Potkin, Steven G., Jessica A. Turner, Guia Guffanti, Anita Lakatos, James H. Fallon, Dana D. Nguyen, Daniel Mathalon, Judith Ford, John Lauriello, and Fabio Macciardi. "A genome-wide association study of schizophrenia using brain activation as a quantitative phenotype." *Schizophrenia Bulletin* 35, no. 1 (2009): 96–108.

Raine, Adrian. "From genes to brain to antisocial behavior." *Current Directions in Psychological Science* 17, no. 5 (2008): 323–328.

Rosell, Daniel R., Judy L. Thompson, Mark Slifstein, Xiaoyan Xu, W. Gordon Frankle, Antonia S. New, Marianne Goodman, et al. "Increased serotonin 2A receptor availability in the orbitofrontal cortex of physically aggressive personality disordered patients." *Biological Psychiatry* 67, no. 12 (2010): 1154–1162.

Saxe, Rebecca, and Anna Wexler. "Making sense of another mind: The role of the right temporo-parietal junction." *Neuropsychologia* 43, no. 10 (2005): 1391–1399.

Shirtcliff, Elizabeth A., Michael J. Vitacco, Alexander R. Graf, Andrew J. Gostisha, Jenna L. Merz, and Carolyn Zahn-Waxler. "Neurobiology of empathy and callousness: Implications for the development of antisocial behavior." *Behavioral Sciences & the Law* 27, no. 2 (2009): 137–171.

Skeem, Jennifer L., and David J. Cooke. "Is criminal behavior a central component of psychopathy? Conceptual directions for resolving the debate." *Psychological Assessment* 22, no. 2 (2010): 433.

Tsankova, Nadia, William Renthal, Arvind Kumar, and Eric J. Nestler. "Epigenetic regulation in psychiatric disorders." *Nature Reviews Neuroscience* 8, no. 5 (2007): 355–367.

Vitacco, Michael J., Craig S. Neumann, and Rebecca L. Jackson. "Testing a four-factor model of psychopathy and its association with ethnicity, gender, intelligence, and violence." *Journal of Consulting and Clinical Psychology* 73, no. 3 (2005): 466.

Wallinius, Märta, Thomas Nilsson, Björn Hofvander, Henrik Anckarsäter, and Gunilla Stålenheim. "Facets of psychopathy among mentally disordered offenders: Clinical comorbidity patterns and prediction of violent and criminal behavior." *Psychiatry Research* 198, no. 2 (2012): 279–284.

Zak, Paul J. "The physiology of moral sentiments." *Journal of Economic Behavior & Organization* 77, no. 1 (2011): 53–65.

For Further Viewing

Discovery Channel's *Curiosity*: "How Evil Are You?" (Eli Roth segment)
http://www.youtube.com/watch?v=En10bS_JW6Y

Discovery Channel's *Through the Wormhole*: "Can We Eliminate Evil?"
https://www.youtube.com/watch?v=Hqb8C9PTcoc

The Moth Radio Hour: "Confessions of a Pro-Social Psychopath"
http://worldsciencefestival.com/videos/moth_confessions_of_a_pro_social_psychopath

NOVA: "Can Science Stop Crime?"
http://www.pbs.org/wgbh/nova/tech/can-science-stop-crime.html

Oslo Freedom Forum: "The Mind of a Dictator"
http://www.psychologytoday.com/blog/engineering-the-brain/201106/the-mind-dictator

ReasonTV: "Three Ingredients for Murder"
http://reason.com/blog/2010/08/19/reasontv-three-ingredients-for

TED: "Exploring the Mind of a Killer"
http://www.ted.com/talks/jim_fallon_exploring_the_mind_of_a_killer.html

World Science Festival: "Madness Redefined"
http://worldsciencefestival.com/webcasts/madness_redefined

Page numbers in *italics* refer to figures.